MaryJane's
CAST IRON
—— KITCHEN ——

MaryJane Butters

MaryJane's
CAST IRON
— KITCHEN —

MaryJane Butters

GIBBS SMITH
TO ENRICH AND INSPIRE HUMANKIND

First Edition
21 20 19 18 17   5 4 3 2 1

Published by
Gibbs Smith
P.O. Box 667
Layton, Utah 84041

1.800.835.4993 orders
Gibbs-Smith.com

Printed and bound in China.

Gibbs Smith books are printed on either recycled, 100% post-consumer waste; FSC-certified papers; or on paper produced from sustainable PEFC-certified forest/controlled wood sources. Learn more at PEFC.org.

ISBN: 978-1-4236-4803-1
Library of Congress Control Number: 2017932670

DEDICATION

Mother
Helen

Granny
Rita Victoria

Great Granny
Hilda Matilda

This book and my love for cast-iron cooking
was made possible by

THE WOMEN BEFORE ME

who loved and cherished their cast-iron cookware.

Let me guess. You've shied away from cast iron because someone spooked you with the words "well-seasoned." Or maybe "rust." Perhaps you thought you needed non-stick cookware just-in-case. If so, I'm here to put a few cast-iron myths to rest and get you started on the road to legendary.

Unlike modern cookware, there isn't much that can ruin cast iron. I dare say we could probably circle the Earth with the discarded high-tech, non-stick pans that were accidently overheated and ruined forever. Or scratched and scarred because special tools weren't used. With scratch-proof cast iron, you merely start over, giving it a new surface. "Good as new again" might be something your great-granny said more than once about the very skillet you have sitting in your attic.

The women of my family brandished cast iron the way a farmer brandishes a pitchfork. My mother's oversized campfire griddle was a source of pride whenever her kids came back to camp carrying a mess of fish they'd caught.

And no doubt, her kitchen skillet, capable of simmering deer steaks in home-canned tomatoes 'til they were fork-tender, gave her yet another boast. "Swiss steak," she'd proclaim after first braising the venison in bacon fat. And her chicken dumplings, fried scones, and raspberry pandowdies were the stuff legends are made of.

In the late '20s, Granny Rita took my mother, Helen, and my aunt, Dorothy, to the outback in a gas-powered carriage. Back then, you didn't worry about the weight of your suitcase; you worried about the weight of too much cast iron—three sizes of skillets, one waffle iron, two griddles, two Dutch ovens, a couple of saucepans, and a fire iron.

Kent, MaryJane, Scott, 1958

catch of the day, 1959

deer hunting, 1959

camping - Helen + Dorothy

And no doubt, I inherited my mother's passion for catching fish.

But more important, I inherited her cast iron that she inherited from her mother, and my daughter will someday inherit from me, and her daughters … on and on. See what I mean? Legendary. It's not just cookware, it's Annie Oakley. Daniel Boone. In a league of its own, no other cookware can come anywhere close to giving you chicken so crisp you'll never think nuggets again or a pot roast so fall-apart tender that no matter how you dice it, you won't be needing to slice it. Or a Dutch baby so perfectly stand-up crisp around the edges yet silky soft in the middle, the lyrics to "Cry Like a Baby" get stuck in your head.

Come on in and apron up. I'm much obliged to be introducing you to your future life partner.

But first, in honor of the outdoorsy clan I come from, I want to head outdoors for a few pages before kitchen duty takes us back inside.

Who doesn't love sitting around a campfire?

Chimeneas and fire bowls are good alternatives if you don't have a place for an outdoor fire pit. A heavy-duty, cast-iron campfire tripod works best with an open bowl.

Helen, 1925

MaryJane, 1956

MaryJane, 1974

MaryJane, Rex, 1960

Batters Family Camp, 1960

Or eating a campfire meal?

I contend people bond better without a roof over their heads. And because I'm always on the lookout for dinners that get everyone involved, pie irons allow each person to make and bake her or his own meal. Now, don't let the "pie" part of these cast-iron devices mislead you. For under $20 each, you can buy waffle, dog 'n' brat, bread 'n' biscuit, panini, round hamburger (I use it to roast chicken breasts), and even square "just about anything including toasted pecans" pie irons for your evening escapades, PieIron.com.

My favorite quick campfire treat is to load my square pie iron with a peanut-butter, banana, and chocolate-bar sandwich. After I unload the warm, gooey goodness onto a plate, I top it with vanilla ice cream.

Old-fashioned waffle irons were designed for use with wood cookstoves by removing one of the round top plates so the base of the iron is in direct contact with the fire. But they can also be used outdoors by tucking campfire coals under the lower compartment. The top part of the waffle iron is designed to swivel and turn above the heat for browning on both sides. Make sure your waffle iron is hot and well-oiled before pouring in the batter. Never place it in open flames. And don't open the iron too soon to peek. When you start to smell the aroma of waffles wafting through the air, they're done.

A camp Dutch oven has three legs and a flanged, snug-fitting lid so it can be set on a bed of hot coals and then loaded with hot coals on top—an outdoor convection oven! It can be used for baking, stewing, and roasting.

Pssst. Don't stop with cookware.
How about a cast-iron truck bed?

Cast-iron tractor
seat stool?

Cast-iron boot puller?

Or how about a...

... cast-iron, claw-foot, outdoor bathtub?

Cast-iron backyard sink?

Can you imagine your great-granny's grin about now?

ONTENTS

Nectarine & Sour-Cream Wedge Cake

Spinach Dip with Panbread Bites

Breadsticks

Swiss Chard Gratin

Mini Apple Pies

Chicken, Bacon & Swiss Hand Pies

Section 5

Baked Peaches

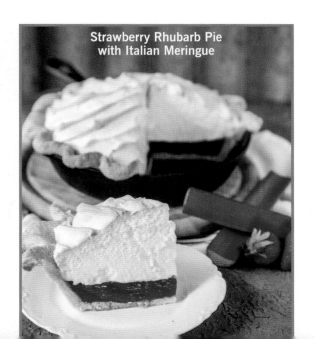

Strawberry Rhubarb Pie
with Italian Meringue

HEART-SHAPED EGGS IN A BLANKET

To serve up some love for breakfast, butter a slice of bread on both sides and set aside. Over low heat, preheat a 10½"-round cast-iron griddle. Once griddle is hot, brush with 1 t melted butter. Place bread on griddle and toast for 1–2 minutes on each side, or until golden brown. Set aside. Lightly butter the inside of a metal, heart-shaped cookie cutter, place on griddle, and crack an egg inside. Once egg is cooked, remove cutter and egg from griddle using a spatula. Remove egg from cookie cutter, and use cookie cutter to cut a heart shape from center of toast. Place fried egg in center of toast; sprinkle with salt and pepper.

8" Cast-Iron Skillet

3   T butter
4   eggs
½   cup flour
½   cup milk or coconut milk
2   T honey
1   t almond extract
¼   t salt
powdered sugar
maple syrup

gluten free

Make it gluten free:
Replace flour with
white rice flour.

 DUTCH BABY

I've made at least one Dutch baby I'll never forget. I was working for the Forest Service while living 27 miles from the end of a dirt road in the heart of the Selway-Bitterroot Wilderness. One of the airplane pilots who brought in supplies and food staples surprised me with a dozen fresh eggs, butter, and two cold beers on ice. I drank the first one while stoking my woodstove and warming up my trusty cast-iron skillet. It seems odd to me now, but a Dutch baby and a cold beer was the best lunch I'd eaten in a long while.

MAKES: 4 SERVINGS

1. Preheat oven to 425°F.

2. In an 8" cast-iron skillet over medium heat, melt butter and distribute evenly. Remove skillet from heat and set aside.

3. In a medium bowl, beat eggs. Add flour, milk, honey, almond extract, and salt; beat until blended but still somewhat lumpy.

4. Pour batter into skillet and bake until puffy on the edges and golden brown, about 15 minutes.

5. Using a fine-mesh sieve, sprinkle with powdered sugar and drizzle with maple syrup.

Cast-Iron Mini-Cake Pan

3   T butter
4   eggs
½   cup flour
½   cup milk or coconut milk
¼   t salt
⅛   t ground nutmeg
powdered sugar
fresh lemon juice

" Lemon tree
very pretty, and
the lemon flavor
is sweet... "
– Brazilian Folk Song

🌱gluten
free

Make it gluten free:
Replace flour with
white rice flour.

MINI DUTCH BABIES

Single-serve Dutch babies ensure that everyone gets plenty of yummy crust. I've served them to B&B guests with butter, sliced bananas, chopped walnuts, and maple syrup before, but my powdered-sugar/lemon-squeeze topping gets a 5-star review every time.

MAKES: 7 MINI DUTCH BABIES

1. Preheat oven to 425°F.

2. Evenly divide butter between cups of a cast-iron mini-cake pan. Place pan in hot oven for 2–3 minutes to melt butter. Remove from oven, brush butter over bottom and sides of each cup; set aside.

3. In a medium bowl, beat eggs. Add flour, milk, salt, and nutmeg; beat until blended but still somewhat lumpy.

4. Evenly divide batter between cake-pan cups, place pan on a large baking sheet (to catch any drips), and bake until puffy on the edges and golden brown, about 15 minutes.

5. Using a fine-mesh sieve, sprinkle with powdered sugar and squeeze fresh lemon juice over the top.

8" Cast-Iron Skillet

SAVORY DUTCH BABY

I have a soft spot for savory breakfasts, and this Dutch baby with caramelized onion sauce offers a nice twist on a classic cast-iron dish. The savory-yet-sweet flavor of the onion sauce is a perfect match for the puffy, creamy Dutch-baby base, and greens add a peppery crunch.

MAKES: 4 SERVINGS

Caramelized Onion Sauce:

2	T olive oil
1	yellow onion, peeled, quartered, and sliced
1	T flour
2	T white wine
½	cup beef broth
½	t fresh thyme
⅛	t salt

Dutch Baby:

3	T butter
4	eggs
½	cup flour
½	cup milk or coconut milk
¼	t salt
watercress	

1. Make sauce: Preheat oil in a medium skillet over medium heat; add onion slices, coating evenly. Cover and cook 15 minutes, stirring occasionally. Remove cover; reduce heat to low. Continue cooking, stirring occasionally, until onions release their sugar and begin to caramelize and turn golden brown.

2. Add flour to onions and mix well. Add wine, cook for 30 seconds, and add beef broth. Continue to cook until sauce has thickened; stir in thyme and salt. Remove skillet from heat and set aside.

3. Make Dutch baby: Preheat oven to 425°F.

4. In an 8" cast-iron skillet over medium heat, melt butter and distribute evenly. Remove skillet from heat and set aside.

5. In a medium bowl, beat eggs. Add flour, milk, and salt. Beat until blended but still somewhat lumpy.

6. Pour batter into skillet and bake until puffy around the edges and golden brown, about 15 minutes,

7. Top with sauce and watercress.

Mushroom Ragout Breakfast

This breakfast dish has it all—creamy polenta and rich, flavorful mushroom ragout, topped with eggs baked right in the sauce. It can also be made the night before, then popped in the oven the next morning for a fuss-free breakfast—just make sure to allow a few extra minutes of cooking time so it comes out of the oven piping hot.

MAKES: 4 SERVINGS

10" Square Cast-Iron Baking Pan

1. Preheat oven to 400°F. Generously butter a 10" square cast-iron baking pan.

2. Make ragout: Melt butter in a large skillet over medium heat. Add mushrooms and garlic; cook, stirring frequently, until mushrooms are tender (about 10 minutes).

3. Add wine to skillet, cook for 30 seconds, and add tomato sauce, diced tomatoes (including liquid), fennel, salt, pepper, and crushed red pepper. Reduce heat to low and continue to simmer, stirring occasionally, for 20 minutes.

4. While ragout is cooking, make polenta: In a medium saucepan over medium heat, bring milk to a simmer. Whisk in polenta and continue to simmer, whisking frequently, until thickened. Add cheeses, parsley, lemon juice, salt, and pepper; mix well.

5. Add polenta to prepared baking pan and smooth out top. Top with mushroom ragout.

6. Make four divots in ragout, each large enough for 1 egg. Crack an egg in each divot, loosely cover baking pan with foil, and bake for 30 minutes. Remove foil and bake an additional 10–12 minutes, or until eggs are set. Just before serving, garnish with parsley and pepper.

Mushroom Ragout:

2	T butter
1½	lbs crimini mushrooms, quartered (about 6 cups)
3	garlic cloves, peeled and minced (about 1 T)
2	T white wine
1	15-oz can tomato sauce
1	14.5-oz can diced tomatoes
½	t fennel seed, lightly crushed
¼	t salt
½	t pepper
¼	t crushed red pepper
4	eggs

Polenta:

3	cups milk
1	cup dry polenta
2½	ozs goat cheese (about ¼ cup)
1	oz Parmesan cheese, shredded (about ¼ cup)
¼	cup fresh parsley, minced, plus more for serving
1	T fresh lemon juice (about 1 lemon)
½	t salt
¼	t pepper, plus more for serving

6-Cavity Cast-Iron Muffin Pan

Ham, Mushroom & Asparagus Mini Quiches

I love the simplicity of single-serve dishes—especially if I'm feeding a crowd. In addition to simplifying the serving process, these mini quiches also bake up in less time than a traditional quiche, which leaves more time for enjoying company over coffee.

MAKES: 6 MINI QUICHES

Crust:

1⅓	cups flour, plus more for dusting
¼	t salt
9	T cold butter
3	T cold water

Filling:

2	t butter
3	crimini mushrooms, halved and sliced (about 3 T)
3	asparagus spears, sliced (about ¼ cup)
1½	ozs cooked ham, finely diced (about ¼ cup)
3	eggs
2	t milk
⅛	t salt
⅛	t pepper
1	T shredded cheddar cheese

1. Make crust: Combine flour and salt in a medium bowl or food processor. Cut in butter until mixture resembles coarse crumbs. Sprinkle in water and blend just until dough forms. Shape into a disc, wrap in plastic wrap, and refrigerate for 30 minutes.

2. Preheat oven to 400°F. Lightly butter a 6-cavity cast-iron muffin pan.

3. On a lightly floured surface, roll the dough to ⅛" thickness. Cut dough into 6" circles and line prepared muffin pan cavities with dough. Shape edges, if desired. Bake for 12–15 minutes, or until outer edges turn golden brown.

4. Make filling: In a medium skillet, melt butter; cook mushrooms and asparagus for about 3 minutes. Remove from heat and stir in ham. Divide filling evenly between shells.

5. In a medium bowl, whisk eggs, milk, salt, and pepper together. Divide egg mixture evenly between shells. Top each quiche with cheese and bake at 400°F for 18–20 minutes, or until eggs are set.

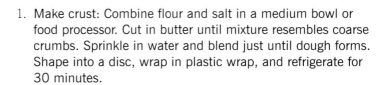

VINTAGE CAST IRON

Muffins, cornbread, cupcakes, mini quiches, and more … your cast-iron muffin pan is a can't-live-without-it kitchen staple. I have four vintage muffin pans; two have six cavities like the one above and two have 11 cavities for larger batches.

6-Cavity Cast-Iron Muffin Pan

2½   ozs extra-sharp Cheddar cheese,
      shredded (about ⅔ cup)
3   ozs feta cheese, crumbled
      (about ⅓ cup)
¼   cup walnuts, coarsely chopped
⅓   cup pesto
½   cup buttermilk
1   egg
2   T butter, melted
¼   t fresh lemon juice
1   cup flour
1¼   t baking powder
¼   t salt

PESTO MUFFINS

These muffins fill the house with an intoxicatingly delicious pesto aroma. Once they're out of the oven and barely cool enough to eat, they often disappear before my eyes—they're *that* good.

MAKES: 6 MUFFINS

1. Preheat oven to 375°F. Line a 6-cavity cast-iron muffin pan with paper liners.

2. In a small bowl, combine cheeses, walnuts, and pesto.

3. In a small bowl, whisk together buttermilk, egg, melted butter, and lemon juice.

4. In a medium bowl, combine flour, baking powder, and salt. Add buttermilk mixture to flour mixture and stir just until blended.

5. Using as few strokes as possible, fold in cheese mixture.

6. Spoon into paper liners until full and well-rounded. (Mixture won't rise much during baking, so mound 'em up!) Bake muffins for 22–25 minutes, or until a toothpick inserted into the center of a muffin comes out clean.

" Pounding fragrant things—particularly garlic, basil, and parsley—is a tremendous antidote to depression ... Pounding these things produces an alteration in one's being—from sighing with fatigue to inhaling with pleasure. **"**

– Patience Gray, cookery author

6-Cavity Cast-Iron Muffin Pan

Ham Muffins

If you're craving something a little salty with a tangy edge, these muffins are for you. I love the pairing of kalamata olives and ham, and find it hard to resist nibbling on an extra olive or two while mixing up the batter.

MAKES: 6 MUFFINS

⅓ cup kalamata olives, chopped (reserve 3 T juice)
3 ozs cooked ham, cut into ¼" cubes (about ½ cup)
2 ozs extra-sharp Cheddar cheese, shredded (about ½ cup)
1 t dried rosemary, crushed
¼ t pepper
⅓ cup buttermilk
1 egg
2 T butter, melted
¼ t fresh lemon juice
1 cup flour
1¼ t baking powder
¼ t salt

Optional: Spice things up a bit by adding 2 T finely chopped fresh poblano pepper and ¼ t red pepper flakes to the olive mixture.

1. Preheat oven to 375°F. Line a 6-cavity cast-iron muffin pan with paper liners.

2. In a small bowl, combine olives, ham, cheese, rosemary, and pepper.

3. In a small bowl, whisk together buttermilk, egg, melted butter, lemon juice, and reserved olive juice.

4. In a medium bowl, combine flour, baking powder, and salt. Add buttermilk mixture to flour mixture and stir just until blended.

5. Using as few strokes as possible, fold in olive mixture.

6. Spoon into paper liners until full and well rounded. (Mixture won't rise much during baking, so mound 'em up!) Bake muffins for 22–25 minutes, or until a toothpick inserted into the center of a muffin comes out clean.

My vintage hand-held, cast-iron lemon squeezer is a beauty. It features a wooden ball that pushes against the top of the lemon and a beautiful perforated porcelain cup that allows the juice to flow through while holding the seeds.

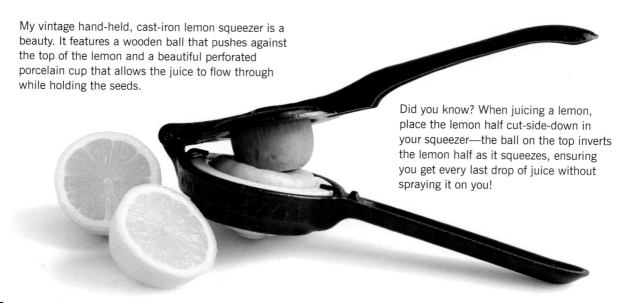

Did you know? When juicing a lemon, place the lemon half cut-side-down in your squeezer—the ball on the top inverts the lemon half as it squeezes, ensuring you get every last drop of juice without spraying it on you!

6-Cavity Cast-Iron Muffin Pan

8	ozs frozen hash browns (about 2 cups), thawed
4	ozs sharp Cheddar cheese, shredded (about 1 cup)
3	slices bacon (about 3 ozs), cooked and diced
2	T flour
2	T minced chives
¼	t salt
⅛	t pepper
6	eggs, divided

salsa (optional)
sour cream (optional)

BACON & EGG CUPS

These cups embody everything I love about breakfast—crisp bacon, perfectly seasoned hash browns, cheese, and fluffy scrambled eggs, all dressed up with a spoonful of fresh salsa.

MAKES: 6 EGG CUPS

1. Preheat oven to 400°F. Generously butter a 6-cavity cast-iron muffin pan.

2. In a medium bowl, combine hash browns, cheese, bacon, flour, chives, salt, and pepper; stir to combine.

3. In a small bowl, gently whisk 1 egg and stir into the hash-brown mixture. Evenly divide mixture between prepared muffin cups. Firmly press mixture into the bottom and up the sides of each muffin cavity.

4. Bake for 30–35 minutes or until hash browns begin to turn golden brown. Let cool for 10 minutes.

5. While hash-brown cups are cooling, whisk together remaining eggs. Generously butter a medium skillet and scramble eggs over medium-low heat.

6. Carefully run a dull knife around the inside of each muffin cup to remove from pan. Evenly divide scrambled eggs between hash-brown cups. If desired, serve with salsa and sour cream.

Fresh from our (wallpapered) henhouse to yours. What a wonderful surprise when our patterns for both children's and adults' egg-gathering aprons sold out the first day we put them up for sale. I mean, who can be without an egg-gathering apron that's also handy for garden produce, notebook and pencil, hankie, or maybe a baby kitten or two?

29

Cast-Iron Aebleskiver Pan

3 eggs
2 cups buttermilk
1 t vanilla extract
2 cups flour
1½ t sugar
½ t salt
1 T baking powder
1 t baking soda
½ t pulverized cardamom seeds
(about 4 pods)
¾ cup safflower oil
powdered sugar

How to roll an aebleskiver:

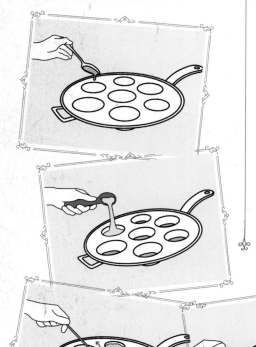

 ASIC AEBLESKIVER

Aebleskiver are round Danish "puff pancakes"—solid like a pancake or griddlecake, but light and fluffy like a popover. The name means, literally, "apple slices," and traditional aebleskiver often contained apples. They are such a part of Danish culture that annual Danish celebrations are often called "Aebleskiver Days."

MAKES: 35 AEBLESKIVER

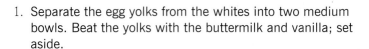

1. Separate the egg yolks from the whites into two medium bowls. Beat the yolks with the buttermilk and vanilla; set aside.

2. In a large bowl, combine flour, sugar, salt, baking powder, baking soda, and cardamom; add yolk-buttermilk mixture and stir well.

3. Beat egg whites until stiff. Carefully fold them into the flour mixture without breaking them down.

4. Place a cast-iron aebleskiver pan on the stove over medium heat. Add 1 t safflower oil to each cup and continue heating for a few minutes.

5. With a spoon, fill each cup with batter about ¾ full. Do not overfill. If the oil is ready, the batter will sizzle when it's dropped. Reduce heat to low.

6. When the aebleskiver are ready to be turned, they will start to bubble and separate from the sides of the pan. (Be patient—this can take several minutes.) At this point, run a dull knife around the inside edges of the cups to make sure they're loose enough to turn. Using a knitting needle, chopstick, or knife, rotate each aebleskiver a quarter turn. Let cook for a minute and continue turning until a ball is formed. After each ball is golden brown, remove from pan with a spoon to a serving plate. Repeat steps 5 & 6 with remaining batter.

7. Add powdered sugar to a fine-mesh sieve. Just before serving, dust aebleskiver with powdered sugar and serve with applesauce and preserves or maple syrup.

VINTAGE CAST IRON

Aebleskiver are cooked on the stovetop in a special cast-iron "skillet" that has several cups with rounded bottoms, allowing you to "roll" the dough for perfect little balls of light-and-puffy goodness.

You might notice that I seem to be talking about one little lone aebleskiver in my recipes. But no ... like the word "moose," the word "aebleskiver" is both singular and plural. (Meese? Mooses?) It's a Danish word that loosely translates to "apple slices," since aebleskiver are traditionally served with apples. The reason my recipe makes 35 is because, if this is your first time making aebleskiver, your first few attempts might not be exactly plateable.

Cast-Iron Aebleskiver Pan

3 eggs
2 cups buttermilk
1 t vanilla extract
2 cups flour
1½ t sugar
½ t salt
1 T baking powder
1 t baking soda
½ t pulverized cardamom seeds
   (about 4 pods)
¾ cup safflower oil
powdered sugar
Cherry Pie Freezer Jam, p. 90

CHERRY AEBLESKIVER

MAKES: 35 AEBLESKIVER

1. Separate the egg yolks from the whites into two medium bowls. Beat the yolks with the buttermilk and vanilla; set aside.

2. In a large bowl, combine flour, sugar, salt, baking powder, baking soda, and cardamom; add yolk-buttermilk mixture and stir well.

3. Beat egg whites until stiff. Carefully fold them into the flour mixture without breaking them down.

4. Place a cast-iron aebleskiver pan on the stove over medium heat. Add 1 t safflower oil to each cup and continue heating for a few minutes.

5. With a spoon, fill each cup with batter about ⅓ full. Quickly add a dollop of Cherry Pie Freezer Jam, p. 90, then cover with a dollop of batter. Do not overfill. If the oil is ready, the batter will sizzle when it's dropped. Reduce heat to low and follow the basic aebleskiver cooking technique as described in step 6 of the Basic Aebleskiver recipe, p. 30.

6. Add powdered sugar to a fine-mesh sieve. Just before serving, dust aebleskiver with powdered sugar and serve with additional cherry preserves.

CHOCOLATE AEBLESKIVER

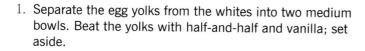

MAKES: 35 AEBLESKIVER

Cast-Iron Aebleskiver Pan

1. Separate the egg yolks from the whites into two medium bowls. Beat the yolks with half-and-half and vanilla; set aside.

2. In a large bowl, combine flour, cocoa powder, sugar, salt, baking powder, baking soda, and cinnamon; add yolk mixture and stir well.

3. Beat egg whites until stiff. Carefully fold them into the flour mixture without breaking them down.

4. Place a cast-iron aebleskiver pan on the stove over medium heat. Add 1 t safflower oil to each cup and continue heating for a few minutes.

5. With a spoon, fill each cup with batter about ¾ full. Do not overfill. If the oil is ready, the batter will sizzle when it's dropped. Reduce heat to low and follow the basic aebleskiver cooking technique as described in step 6 of the Basic Aebleskiver recipe, p. 30.

6. Add powdered sugar to a fine-mesh sieve. Just before serving, dust aebleskiver with powdered sugar and serve with whipped cream.

3	eggs
2	cups half-and-half
1	t vanilla extract
1⅔	cups flour
⅓	cup cocoa powder
2	t sugar
½	t salt
1	T baking powder
1	t baking soda
½	t cinnamon
¾	cup safflower oil
	powdered sugar
	whipped cream

Cast-Iron Aebleskiver Pan

7   3¼"-round slices
      Canadian bacon
2   T finely diced red bell pepper
1   T finely diced zucchini
1   egg
½   t milk
½   oz sharp Cheddar cheese,
      shredded (about 2 T)

gluten free

Canadian-Bacon Mini Quiches

I love dreaming up new ways to serve dishes traditionally made with crusts. This particular recipe transforms an ordinary piece of Canadian bacon into a bite-sized crust that is tender with just the right amount of crispness around the edges.

MAKES: 7 MINI QUICHES

1. Preheat oven to 400°F.

2. Line cups of a cast-iron aebleskiver pan with a slice of Canadian bacon, pinching in each slice so it makes a bowl in the half-round cup of the pan.

3. Evenly divide pepper and zucchini between Canadian-bacon bowls.

4. In a small bowl, combine egg, milk, and salt; evenly divide mixture between Canadian-bacon bowls.

5. Bake for 15–18 minutes, or until egg mixture has set. Remove pan from oven, sprinkle tops with cheese, and bake 2 more minutes, or until cheese is melted.

Cast-Iron Waffle Iron

2   T coconut oil, melted
4   eggs, room temperature
¼   cup applesauce, room temperature
1   t almond extract
¼   t sea salt
1   t baking soda
½   t apple-cider vinegar
2   cups almond flour
maple syrup

gluten free

Because store-bought almond flour can sit on the shelf too long and go rancid, I make my own, using a food processor.

ALMOND WAFFLES

When I'm in the mood for something sweet and simple for breakfast, nothing beats these almond waffles. I love the smell of waffles cooking in the morning, and the scent of almond as the waffles cook adds an extra layer of enjoyment to the process.

MAKES: 4 SERVINGS

1. In a large bowl, whisk together the oil, eggs, applesauce, almond extract, salt, baking soda, and vinegar. Add almond flour and whisk just until smooth.

2. Preheat a cast-iron waffle iron over medium heat.

3. Once the waffle iron is hot, brush with coconut oil. Spoon about ¼ of the batter into the waffle iron. Cook for about 2½ minutes on each side or until golden. Repeat with remaining batter.

4. Serve waffles with butter and maple syrup.

VINTAGE CAST IRON

Cast-iron waffle irons are designed so that you can flip them over on the stovetop for browning on both sides. Make sure your waffle iron is hot and well-oiled before pouring in the batter. Never place in open flames. And don't open the iron too soon to peek. When you start to smell the aroma of waffles wafting through the air, they're done.

Serve up some love for breakfast, lunch, or dinner with a heart-shaped waffle iron like my vintage beauty with pink, early Bakelite handles.

Cast-Iron Waffle Iron

Potato & Buckwheat Waffles:

12	ozs potatoes, peeled and diced (about 2¼ cups)
2	cloves garlic, peeled
1	bay leaf
¼	cup olive oil
¾	cup buttermilk
¼	cup buckwheat flour
3	eggs
½	t salt
¼	t caraway seeds
1	t baking powder
½	t baking soda
coconut oil	

Cabbage & Fennel Hash:

8	ozs andouille sausage, cooked and sliced into ¼" coins
½	cup barbecue sauce
1½	T olive oil
12	ozs green cabbage, shredded (about 2½ cups)
½	cup purple cabbage, shredded
½	fennel bulb, trimmed and shredded (about 1 cup)
¼	onion, peeled and shredded (about ½ cup)
½	t salt
½	t pepper

SAVORY POTATO & BUCKWHEAT WAFFLES

This recipe offers a wonderfully unique twist on waffles. The potatoes give the waffles a moist, tender base, and the buckwheat and caraway complement each other perfectly. The cabbage, fennel, andouille sausage, and barbecue sauce toppings make it a truly memorable dish.

MAKES: 4 WAFFLES

1. Place potatoes, garlic cloves, and bay leaf into a 4-qt saucepan. Fill pan with enough water to cover the potatoes and bring to a boil over high heat.

2. Reduce heat to simmer. Once potatoes are fork tender, drain off the water and discard the bay leaf.

3. Add olive oil and buttermilk. Using a potato masher, mash the potatoes until they have a smooth, creamy consistency.

4. Add buckwheat flour, eggs, salt, caraway, baking powder, and baking soda. Mix well.

5. Preheat a cast-iron waffle iron over medium-high heat.

6. Once the waffle iron is hot, brush with coconut oil. Spoon about ¼ of the batter into waffle iron. Cook for about 2½ minutes on each side or until golden. Repeat with remaining batter.

7. Serve with Cabbage and Fennel Hash.

CABBAGE & FENNEL HASH

MAKES: TOPPING FOR 4 WAFFLES

1. In a 2-qt saucepan, heat sausage and barbecue sauce. Set aside.

2. In a large skillet, heat olive oil over medium heat. Add remaining ingredients.

3. Cook for 3–5 minutes, stirring frequently, until cabbage is tender-crisp.

4. Top waffles with cabbage mixture, then sausage.

Did you know that waffles and pancakes are best when made using whole-grain flour? That's because the high amount of gluten in white flour makes them more sticky. Plus, you don't have to worry about over-mixing the batter when you use whole grain.

This nifty vintage cast-iron coffee grinder attaches to your table. You can also use it to grind nuts. This one's marked "made in England." I love to think of a proper British lady kicking aside all that tea and grinding up a cup of joe.

Cast-Iron Grill/Griddle

1   large russet potato (about 1 lb)
3   T safflower oil, divided
¾   t salt
½   t pepper
¼   t paprika
¼   t granulated onion

Special Equipment:

Spiralizer

HASH-BROWN PATTIES

Have you ever diced up potatoes for breakfast, tossed them in a skillet with a little oil, and cooked them for what seems like forever, only to end up with a batch of undercooked potatoes? Disappointing, right? But once I started using my spiralizer to make these hash-brown patties, I bid adieu to undercooked, starchy potatoes, and happily welcomed these crisp, flavorful patties to my breakfast table.

MAKES: 6 PATTIES

1. Using a spiralizer, cut potato into noodles using noodle blade.

2. Using a knife, cut potatoes into manageable lengths and transfer to large bowl. Add 1 T safflower oil, salt, pepper, paprika, and onion to potatoes. Toss to combine.

3. Preheat a cast-iron griddle over medium-low heat. Once griddle is hot, add 1 T safflower oil. Add potatoes in mounds (roughly ¾ cup for each mound). Spread out each mound and flatten with the back side of a spatula. Cook for 4–5 minutes, flip over and cook an additional 4–5 minutes.

4. Repeat this process with remaining potato mixture, adding remaining safflower oil as needed. Serve hash-brown patties immediately.

Cast-Iron Grill/Griddle

Sausage, Zucchini & Hash-Brown Biscuits

Sometimes, simplicity wins out, and nothing sounds more appetizing than a classic buttermilk biscuit sandwich. Just mix up a little sausage with zucchini, hash browns, and garlic; fry it up on your trusty cast-iron griddle; and top with cheese. A comforting classic is ready for the taking.

MAKES: 8 BISCUITS

Biscuits:

1   full batch Buttermilk
    Biscuits, p. 88

Sausage Patties:

1   lb breakfast sausage
1   zucchini, shredded
    (about ¾ cup)
4   ozs frozen hash browns, thawed
    (about 1 cup)
2   garlic cloves, peeled and
    minced (about 2 t)
¼   t pepper
4   ozs Cheddar cheese, sliced

1. Prepare a full batch of Buttermilk Biscuits, p. 88.

2. In a medium bowl, combine sausage, zucchini, hash browns, garlic, and pepper. Form into 8 patties.

3. Heat a cast-iron griddle over medium heat. Cook patties for 6–7 minutes, flip over, and cook for an additional 5 minutes. Top with cheese, and continue to cook until cheese is melted.

4. Serve sausage patties on Buttermilk Biscuits.

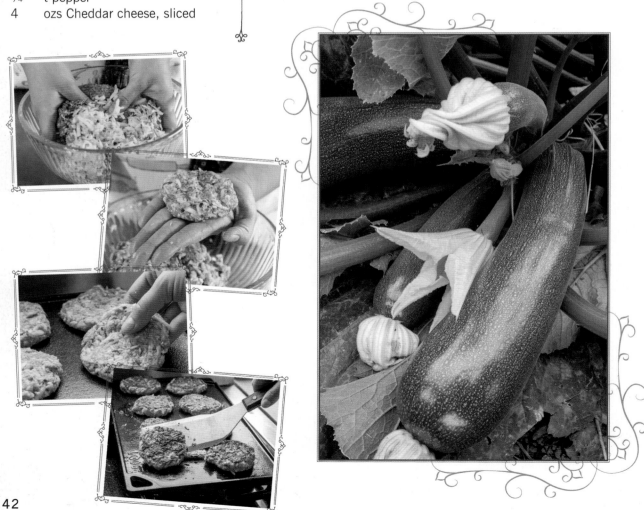

SAVORY STRATA

1   T butter
4   ozs crimini mushrooms, halved and sliced (about 1 cup)
3   cups 1" day-old baguette cubes
½   lb Italian sausage links, cooked, quartered, and sliced
4   ozs cherry tomatoes, quartered (about ¾ cup)
3   green onions, sliced (about ½ cup), plus more for garnish
3   ozs crumbled feta cheese (about ⅓ cup)
3   eggs
⅓   cup milk
2   ozs Cheddar cheese, shredded (about ½ cup)

Of all the dishes in my breakfast repertoire, this one is my go-to recipe. I've turned to it more times than I can count. The winning combination of sausage, tomatoes, feta, and green onions has never let me down.

MAKES: 4 SERVINGS

1. Generously butter a 10" square cast-iron baking pan.

2. Add butter to another medium skillet and sauté mushrooms over medium heat until tender (about 5 minutes). Add mushrooms to a medium bowl.

3. Add baguette cubes, sausage, tomatoes, green onions, and feta to bowl with mushrooms. Toss to combine. Add to prepared baking pan.

4. In a medium bowl, whisk eggs and milk together. Pour over bread mixture. Using a spatula, press ingredients down into liquid.

5. Cover with plastic wrap and refrigerate overnight.

6. Remove strata from refrigerator 30 minutes prior to baking. Preheat oven to 350°F.

7. Remove plastic wrap, cover with aluminum foil, and bake 45 minutes. Remove foil, top with Cheddar cheese, and bake an additional 15 minutes. If desired, garnish with green onions.

Alternatively, prepare single-serve stratas in four enameled cast-iron round mini cocottes: Generously butter cocottes and place on a large baking sheet. Evenly divide bread and egg mixtures between cocottes, cover with plastic wrap, and refrigerate overnight. Remove stratas from refrigerator 30 minutes prior to baking. Preheat oven to 350°F. Bake, uncovered, for 35 minutes. If desired, garnish with green onions.

10" Square Cast-Iron Baking Pan

Optional: Enameled Cast-Iron Mini Round Cocotte
(Note: this recipe calls for 4 cocottes)

SWEET STRATA

This dish always gets rave reviews from our B&B guests. It's a regular on our breakfast menu because it's something we can prep the night before and then pop into the oven the next morning. Just make sure you use good quality organic baguettes. The maple cream syrup has a unique flavor—a cross between something caramel-y and maple-y that's as smooth as ice cream melting in your mouth.

MAKES: 4 SERVINGS

1. Generously butter a 10" square cast-iron baking pan.

2. In a medium bowl, combine baguette cubes, cream cheese, and blueberries; add to prepared baking pan.

3. In a small bowl, combine eggs, milk, and syrup. Pour over bread mixture. Using a spatula, press ingredients down into liquid.

4. Cover with plastic wrap and refrigerate overnight.

5. Remove strata from refrigerator 30 minutes prior to baking. Preheat oven to 350°F.

6. Remove plastic wrap, cover with aluminum foil, and bake for 35 minutes.

7. Remove foil and bake until top is golden brown and mixture is set in the center, about 15 minutes.

8. Serve topped with Maple Cream Syrup.

Alternatively, prepare single-serve stratas in four enameled cast-iron round mini cocottes: Generously butter cocottes and place on a large baking sheet. Evenly divide bread and egg mixtures between cocottes, cover with plastic wrap and refrigerate overnight. Remove stratas from refrigerator 30 minutes prior to baking. Preheat oven to 350°F. Bake, uncovered, for 25 minutes. Serve topped with Maple Cream Syrup.

MAPLE CREAM SYRUP

MAKES: 4 SERVINGS

1. In a small saucepan, combine maple syrup and cream. Stir over medium heat until thickened, approximately 15 minutes. Drizzle over strata.

Sweet Strata:

3	cups 1" day-old baguette cubes
2	ozs cream cheese (about ¼ cup), cut into ½" cubes
¼	cup fresh or thawed frozen blueberries
3	eggs
½	cup milk
1½	T maple syrup

10" Square Cast-Iron Baking Pan

Optional: Enameled Cast-Iron Mini Round Cocotte
(Note: this recipe calls for 4 cocottes)

Maple Cream Syrup:

½	cup maple syrup
1	cup heavy cream

10¼" Cast-Iron Skillet

2½ lbs potatoes, unpeeled
4 t safflower oil, divided
2 t butter, divided
1 t salt
4 rosemary sprigs, de-stemmed and minced (about 2 t)
2 T milk
8 oz sliced or shredded cheese, such as Swiss, Emmentaler, Gruyère, raclette, Appenzeller, or Cheddar)

gluten free

Roesti
(SWISS POTATO CAKE)

Roesti is a simple dish with many variations. Usually, the potatoes need to be cooked at least one day beforehand. Sometimes they are shredded raw. In either case, they are pressed together in the skillet to make a compacted cake. Roesti must not be stirred while cooking; it must be able to form its signature golden-brown crust.

MAKES: 6 SERVINGS

1. The day before, boil or bake potatoes until semi-tender. Cool completely and refrigerate.

2. The next day, peel potatoes, if desired, and shred.

3. Heat 2 t safflower oil and 1 t butter over medium heat in a 10¼" cast-iron skillet. Spread potatoes evenly in the skillet and sprinkle with salt and rosemary. Using a large spatula, firmly press into a round cake. Sprinkle with milk.

4. Reduce heat to medium-low when potatoes begin to sizzle. Cook slowly, periodically pressing down with spatula, approximately 20 minutes or until a nice brown crust forms. Loosen with spatula, place platter or flat pan over skillet, and quickly turn upside down. Add remaining 2 t safflower oil and 1 t butter to skillet. Slide Roesti back into skillet, cooked side up.

5. Top with cheese and cover until cheese is melted and bubbly and bottom of Roesti is also browned. Cut into wedges and serve.

10¼" Cast-Iron Skillet

Dough:

1⅓	cups buttermilk
1	T honey
1	T butter, cut into pieces
½	t salt
1	package active dry yeast (about 2¼ t)
3	cups flour, plus more for dusting

Filling:

⅓	cup sugar
2	t cinnamon
¼	t ground nutmeg
4	T butter, softened

Frosting:

3	T butter, softened
3	T heavy cream
¼	t vanilla extract
1	cup powdered sugar

GIANT CINNAMON ROLL

Decadent, swoon-worthy, heavenly … oh, sorry, my mind trailed off while thinking about this cinnamon roll. I can list adjectives all day in an effort to describe this sweet treat, but I fear they won't do it justice. After all, is there anything better than a huge, soft cinnamon roll smothered in frosting?

MAKES: 6 SERVINGS

1. Make dough: In a small saucepan, combine buttermilk, honey, butter, and salt. Over medium-low heat, whisk mixture until honey is dissolved and butter begins to melt (mixture shouldn't feel hot on the inside of your wrist). Remove from heat, whisk in yeast, and set aside.

2. Add flour to a stand mixer fitted with a dough hook. Make a depression in the center of the flour to receive the liquid; add buttermilk mixture to flour.

3. Mix until dough forms, and continue to mix until dough is smooth and pliable (5–8 minutes).

4. Lightly butter a medium bowl. Dust hands and dough with flour and shape into a ball. Place in prepared bowl, cover with plastic wrap, and let rise in a warm place for 1½ hours, or until doubled in bulk.

5. Prepare filling: In a small bowl, combine sugar, cinnamon, and nutmeg; set aside.

6. Preheat oven to 350°F. Generously butter a 10¼" cast-iron skillet.

7. Deflate dough. On a lightly floured surface, roll dough into a 12" x 15" rectangle. Spread 4 T softened butter over dough and cover with filling mixture.

8. From the 15" side, cut the dough into ten 1½" x 12" strips. Roll one strip up, jelly-roll style, into a cinnamon roll. Place in the center of the prepared skillet. Wrap remaining strips, one at a time, around center cinnamon roll to form one large cinnamon roll. Cover with plastic wrap and let rise in a warm place for 30 minutes.

9. After 30 minutes, remove plastic wrap and bake cinnamon roll for 25–30 minutes, or until internal temperature reaches 200–205°F.

10. While cinnamon roll is baking, prepare frosting: In a medium bowl, combine butter, cream, and vanilla. Add about half of the powdered sugar and blend until smooth. Add remaining powdered sugar and blend until smooth and creamy.

11. After cinnamon roll has finished baking, remove from oven, cool for 30 minutes, spread frosting over top, and serve.

SECTION 2
LUNCH & SIDES

Meet my sweetheart Jersey, Ester Lily. We all know how much people fall in love with their dogs, cats, and horses, but to love a cow as passionately as I love Ester Lily (and also Anna, M'lady, Miss Daisy, Magnolia, and Lacy Lou) is the ultimate love affair because my pets also feed my family milk, cream, butter, cheese, and yogurt without fail. Life on a farm is m-m-m-m-m tasty good. Find out just how tasty in my *Milk Cow Kitchen* book that is one part cheese making and one part cow care.

10½" Cast-Iron Griddle

36   button mushrooms
      (about 1¼ lbs)
4   ozs prosciutto, diced
1   red bell pepper, seeded and
      diced (about 1¼ cups)
2   garlic cloves, peeled and
      minced (about 2 t)
¾   cup chicken broth
¼   t salt
2   T dry polenta
1½   ozs shredded Parmesan cheese
      (about ⅓ cup)
1   oz shredded Asiago cheese
      (about ¼ cup)
¼   cup fresh parsley, minced, plus
      more for garnish

PROSCIUTTO & POLENTA STUFFED MUSHROOMS

I'm always excited about stuffed mushrooms, but I especially love a batch of perfectly cooked mushrooms with a simple, yet beautiful, presentation. My round cast-iron griddle does a fantastic job of cooking the mushrooms to perfection, and you can serve the mushrooms right from the pan.

MAKES: 36 MUSHROOMS

1. Preheat oven to 350°F.

2. Remove stems from mushrooms and place the tops gill side up on a 10½" cast-iron griddle (if desired, reserve the stems for use in other dishes); set aside.

3. In a large skillet over medium heat, cook prosciutto for 5 minutes, stirring frequently. Add bell pepper and garlic. Cook an additional 3–5 minutes, stirring frequently, until pepper is tender-crisp.

4. Add chicken broth and salt to skillet; bring to a simmer. Add polenta, mix well, reduce heat to low and cover. Continue to simmer for 5–8 minutes, until polenta is cooked; remove from heat.

5. Divide mixture among mushroom caps.

6. In a small bowl, combine cheeses and parsley. Sprinkle over the tops of the mushrooms and bake for 18–20 minutes, or until mushrooms are tender. Garnish with parsley.

10½" Cast-Iron Griddle

1   lb breakfast sausage
1   cup breadcrumbs
2   eggs
1   red bell pepper, seeded and
    finely diced (about 1¼ cups)
2   garlic cloves, peeled and
    minced (about 2 t)
2   T fresh parsley, minced (about
    1 T), plus more for garnish
½   t pepper
5   ozs Cheddar cheese, cut into
    20 cubes

Sausage & Cheddar Meatballs

These meatballs have a little surprise—as you shape them, you place a square of Cheddar cheese in the center of each. The little pocket of cheese on the inside is wonderful, and all that melted, slightly crisp cheese on the pan just begs to be devoured.

MAKES: 20 MEATBALLS

1. Preheat oven to 400°F.

2. In a medium bowl, combine sausage, breadcrumbs, eggs, bell pepper, garlic, parsley, and pepper.

3. Divide mixture into 20 equal portions. Place a cube of cheese in the center of each portion and roll into balls.

4. Place meatballs on a 10½" round cast-iron griddle and bake for 25 minutes, or until cooked through. Garnish with minced parsley and serve.

10½" Cast-Iron Griddle

Topping:

2	14.5-oz cans diced tomatoes, drained
½	cup red wine
6	garlic cloves, peeled and minced (about 2 T)
½	t salt
¼	t pepper
½	t Italian seasoning
1	t brown sugar
8	ozs mozzarella cheese, sliced
1	oz Parmesan cheese, shredded (about ¼ cup)

Fried Eggplant:

2	Japanese eggplants
2	T fresh lemon juice (about 1 lemon)
¾	t salt, divided
1	cup breadcrumbs
1	oz Parmesan cheese, shredded (about ¼ cup)
¼	cup fresh basil leaves, minced
4	garlic cloves, peeled and minced (about 4 t)
¼	t pepper
2	eggs
6	T safflower oil, divided

Steamed Brussels Sprouts:

12	ozs Brussels sprouts, quartered (about 4 cups)
¼	cup olive oil
2	t lemon juice
½	t salt
½	t pepper
1	T Dijon mustard
¼	t red pepper flakes

Eggplant Parmesan Rounds

Of all the plants I grow in my garden, eggplant is one that always catches my eye. I love the look of the lush, green plants with the glossy, deep-purple eggplants poking out from behind the leaves. I love this dish because the ingredients meld together to create a flavor that just screams summer. Each time I make it, I gain an even deeper appreciation for my cast-iron griddle that transitions seamlessly between stovetop, oven, and table.

MAKES: ABOUT 36 ROUNDS

1. Make topping: Combine diced tomatoes, wine, garlic, salt, pepper, Italian seasoning, and brown sugar in a medium saucepan. Cook over medium-low heat until wine is reduced, about 15 minutes. Remove from heat and set aside.

2. Meanwhile, make fried eggplant: Cut eggplant into ¼"-thick rounds and arrange in a single layer on a baking sheet. Brush with 1 T lemon juice, sprinkle with ¼ t salt, flip over, brush with 1 T lemon juice, and sprinkle with ¼ t salt. Set aside.

3. Combine breadcrumbs, Parmesan, basil, garlic, pepper, and remaining ¼ t salt in a medium bowl. Whisk eggs together in a small bowl.

4. Pat the eggplant dry with paper towels, flip over, and pat the other side dry. Dip eggplant rounds in egg, then coat in breadcrumb mixture.

5. Heat 3 T oil on a 10½" cast-iron griddle over medium-high heat. Fry breaded eggplant rounds for 3–4 minutes on each side, or until golden brown, adding remaining oil as needed.

6. Divide sliced mozzarella between eggplant rounds, then divide the tomato mixture evenly among the rounds; top with Parmesan. Broil until mozzarella is melted.

Steamed Brussels Sprouts

MAKES: 4 SERVINGS

1. Fill a large pot with 2" of water; bring to a boil. Place steamer basket with Brussels sprouts in the pot; cover and steam for 12–15 minutes.

2. In an 8" cast-iron skillet, heat olive oil until warm; add lemon juice, salt, pepper, mustard, and red pepper flakes; mix well. Add Brussels sprouts; toss to coat.

> " ... two steps farther, and I could look down into the **vegetable garden** enclosed within its tall pale of reeds—rich chocolate **earth studded emerald green,** frothed with the whites of cauliflower, jeweled with the **purple globes of eggplant** and the scarlet wealth of tomatoes. "
> – Doris Lessing

10" Square Cast-Iron Baking Pan

Roasted Chicken & Squash:

4	bone-in chicken thighs (about 1½–2 lbs)
3	garlic cloves, peeled and minced (about 1 T)
1	t salt
½	t paprika
¼	t pepper
1	T olive oil
3½	lbs buttercup or butternut squash, peeled, seeded and cut into ½" cubes (about 7 cups)

Herbed Honey Mustard:

¼	cup buttermilk
2	T Dijon mustard
2	T honey
1	T parsley, minced, plus more for garnish.
1	rosemary sprig, de-stemmed and minced (about ½ t)

gluten free

ROASTED CHICKEN & SQUASH WITH HERBED HONEY MUSTARD

This dish makes a wonderfully simple, yet delicious, weeknight meal. The chicken thighs are lightly seared, placed on a bed of squash, and baked. As the chicken cooks, the drippings flavor the squash. The honey-mustard sauce adds a tangy-sweet twist.

MAKES: 4 SERVINGS

1. Preheat oven to 400°F. Generously butter a 10" square cast-iron baking pan.

2. Make roasted chicken and squash: Place chicken thighs on a plate.

3. In a small bowl, combine garlic, salt, paprika, and pepper. Sprinkle over chicken and rub all over surface of thighs.

4. In a medium skillet over medium heat, heat olive oil. Once oil is hot, add chicken thighs, skin side down. Cook for 5 minutes, flip over, and cook an additional 5 minutes; remove from heat.

5. Add about ¾ of the squash to prepared baking pan and place chicken thighs over squash. Add remaining squash, cover with aluminum foil, and bake for 30 minutes. Remove foil and bake an additional 20 minutes, or until internal temperature of the thighs reaches 165°F.

6. Make honey mustard: In a small bowl, combine buttermilk, mustard, honey, parsley, and rosemary. Mix well. Cover and refrigerate until ready to use.

7. Once chicken is ready, sprinkle with fresh minced parsley for garnish and serve with Herbed Honey Mustard.

6-Cavity Cast-Iron Muffin Pan

Chicken Puffs:

1	T coconut oil
4	ozs boneless, skinless chicken breasts
3	cloves garlic, peeled and minced (about 1 T)
½	t red pepper flakes
½	t salt, divided
⅓	cup slivered almonds
4	dates, pitted and finely minced (about ⅓ cup)
4	t lemon juice, divided
½	cup flour
¼	t nutmeg
¼	t cinnamon
½	cup coconut milk
2	eggs

Onion Sauce:

1	T coconut oil
½	medium red onion, diced
1	T cornstarch
1	cup chicken broth
3	dates, pitted and finely minced (about ¼ cup)
1	T lemon juice
1½	t distilled white vinegar
1	t brown sugar
¼	t nutmeg
¼	t cinnamon

CHICKEN PUFFS WITH ONION SAUCE

The base of each puff is reminiscent of a popover with subtle cinnamon-nutmeg notes. The topping is a delectable combination of chicken, almonds, and dates, all dressed up with a tangy onion sauce. This combination of flavors is a great way to add some interest to your midday meal.

MAKES: 6 PUFFS

1. Preheat oven to 425°F. Lightly butter cups of a 6-cavity cast-iron muffin pan.

2. Prepare chicken puffs: In a small skillet over medium heat, heat coconut oil. Once oil is hot, add chicken breasts and cook on each side for 6 minutes. Add garlic, red pepper flakes, and ¼ t salt; cover and cook an additional 6–8 minutes, or until internal temperature reaches 165°F.

3. Remove chicken from skillet and set aside to cool. Add almonds to skillet and sauté until golden brown, stirring frequently; remove from skillet and set aside to cool.

4. Finely dice chicken and add to a medium bowl. Mix in almonds, dates, and 2 t lemon juice.

5. In another medium bowl, combine flour, nutmeg, cinnamon, and remaining ¼ t salt.

6. In a small bowl, combine coconut milk, eggs, and remaining 2 t lemon juice; add to flour mixture and combine until mixed thoroughly (batter will be slightly lumpy).

7. Divide batter evenly between cups in prepared muffin pan. Evenly divide chicken mixture between cups. Place muffin pan on a large baking sheet to catch drips, cover with aluminum foil, and bake for 10 minutes. Remove foil and bake an additional 5 minutes, or until edges are golden brown and batter is cooked through.

8. Prepare onion sauce: In a small saucepan over medium heat, heat coconut oil. Add onion and sauté until translucent, about 5 minutes; add cornstarch and mix well. Add remaining ingredients and continue to cook over medium heat, stirring occasionally until thickened, about 5 minutes. Serve over puffs.

36-oz Cast-Iron Oval Serving Dish

4	lbs Swiss chard
3	T butter
½	onion, peeled and diced (about 1 cup)
3	garlic cloves, peeled and minced (about 1 T)
1	t salt
½	t pepper
¼	t nutmeg
2	T flour
2¼	cups milk
5	ozs Gruyère cheese, shredded and divided (about 1¼ cups)

SWISS-CHARD GRATIN

I can't get enough of the earthy, almost musky flavor of chard. I frequently sauté it with some garlic, olive oil, apple-cider vinegar, and a generous sprinkle of black pepper and call it dinner. But sometimes, we all need a little decadence, and that's what this dish is. When baked in cast iron, the edges of the gratin turn a perfect golden-brown and are, in my opinion, the best part of the dish.

MAKES: 8 SERVINGS

1. Fill a large stockpot with water, leaving about 5" of room at the top. Bring water to a boil. Wash chard and remove stems, reserving about a third of the stems and discarding the rest.

2. When water begins to boil, prepare an ice-water bath in a large bowl. Add chard to the boiling water and cook for 2–3 minutes. (The color of the chard will brighten, but it should still have a little crispness to it.) Transfer chard immediately to the ice-water bath.

3. Line a colander with a thin dishtowel and pour chard into colander. Let water drain off, and then gather the edges of the cloth and wring out as much water as you can from the chard. You should end up with a firm ball. Transfer to a cutting board and slice the ball lengthwise into 1" sections, and then crosswise into 1" sections. Set aside.

4. Preheat oven to 400°F. Lightly butter a 36-oz cast-iron serving dish.

5. Dice the reserved stems and add to a large skillet, along with butter, onion, garlic, salt, pepper, and nutmeg.

6. Sauté over medium heat for about 5 minutes. Stir in flour and cook for about 1 minute. Reduce heat to medium low and slowly add milk, mixing well. Cook until milk has thickened and begins to bubble, stirring frequently. Add about ¾ cup of Gruyère, reserving the other ½ cup for the top. Stir mixture until the cheese has melted, then turn off the heat and mix in the prepared chard. Pour into prepared serving dish, and top with remaining cheese.

7. Bake for 15–20 minutes, or until sides are bubbling and cheese has browned.

Cast-Iron Warmer

Cast-Iron Mini-Cake Pan

CHICKEN, BACON & SWISS HAND PIES

With its great versatility, this mini-cake pan is another of my favorite cast-iron pans. For this particular dish, I would be hard-pressed to find a pan that makes perfectly sized hand pies with such a wonderfully browned crust. These hand pies are great as a make-ahead meal that you can grab-and-go.

MAKES: 7 PIES

Crust:

1¾	cups flour, plus more for dusting
1	t baking powder
¾	t baking soda
¼	t salt
4	T cold butter
1	cup buttermilk

Filling:

4	ozs bacon (about 4 slices), diced
1½	lbs boneless, skinless chicken breasts, diced
¼	t salt
¼	t pepper
8	ozs Swiss cheese, shredded (about 1 cup)
2	ozs kale, coarsely diced (about 2 cups)

1. Preheat oven to 400°F. Lightly butter a cast-iron mini-cake pan.

2. Make crust: In a medium bowl, combine flour, baking powder, baking soda, and salt. Cut in butter until mixture resembles coarse crumbs. Add buttermilk and stir until dough forms.

3. Dust work surface with flour and roll dough to ⅛" thickness. Cut dough into seven 6" squares and line each cup of prepared mini-cake pan with a square.

4. Make filling: In a medium skillet, cook bacon over medium heat for about 5 minutes. Add chicken, salt, and pepper. Continue to cook over medium heat until bacon is crispy and chicken is cooked.

5. Transfer chicken mixture to a medium bowl, draining off any fat. Add Swiss cheese and kale; stir to combine.

6. Divide mixture evenly between mini-cake pan cups and wrap dough over top. Bake for 30 minutes, or until crust is golden brown.

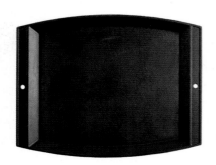

15" x 12¼" Cast-Iron Rectangular Griddle

Spinach Dip:

2	T butter
½	medium sweet white onion, peeled and finely diced (about 1 cup)
3	garlic cloves, peeled and minced (about 1 T)
10	ozs frozen spinach, thawed and squeezed dry
6	ozs shredded Gruyère cheese (about 1½ cups), divided
8	ozs cream cheese (about 1 cup), softened
⅔	cup sour cream
⅓	cup pine nuts
¾	t salt
½	t pepper

Panbread:

2¼	cups flour, plus more for dusting
1½	t baking powder
¾	t baking soda
¾	t salt
1½	T olive oil
1½	T honey
¾	cup warm water
1	t butter, melted

SPINACH DIP WITH PANBREAD BITES

With its eye-catching presentation and fuss-free serving, this dish begs to be made for your next get-together. Did I mention that it's delicious?

MAKES: 10–12 SERVINGS

1. Make spinach dip: In a medium skillet over medium heat, cook butter, onion, and garlic until onion is soft; remove from heat.

2. Add spinach, 1 cup Gruyère, cream cheese, sour cream, pine nuts, salt, pepper, and onion mixture to a food processor; pulse until smooth.

3. Lightly butter a 15" x 12¼" cast-iron griddle. Preheat oven to 425°F.

4. Spread spinach dip in a smooth layer onto cast-iron griddle; set aside.

5. Make panbread: In a medium bowl, combine flour, baking powder, baking soda, and salt; make a well in the center.

6. In a small bowl, combine oil, honey, and water. Pour water into flour mixture and stir until blended (add more flour or water, if needed, to make the dough tacky, but not sticky).

7. Divide dough into 34 small pieces and shape each piece into an oval, dusting with flour as needed. Line sides of pan with shaped bread. Brush with melted butter.

8. Sprinkle remaining ½ cup Gruyère over spinach dip and bake for 15–18 minutes, or until spinach dip is bubbling and bread is golden brown.

Crown jewel? Nope, just an early morning drop of dew on one of our spinach plants.

9-oz Cast-Iron Oval Mini-Server
(Note: this recipe calls for 8 mini-servers)

2	lbs potatoes, halved and sliced into 1/4"-thick slices
4	T butter, divided
1/8	t salt
1/8	t pepper
4	garlic cloves, peeled and minced (about 4 t)
4	T fresh parsley, minced
1	oz sharp Cheddar cheese, shredded (about 1/4 cup)
2	ozs Parmesan cheese, shredded (about 1/2 cup)
1	oz Gruyère cheese, shredded (about 1/4 cup)
1/2	cup heavy cream

gluten free

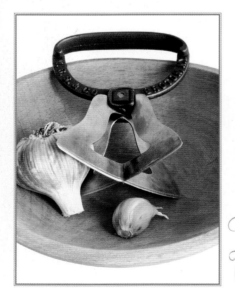

Vintage Cast-Iron Food Chopper

PARMESAN & GARLIC SINGLE-SERVE BRUNCH POTATOES

I was trying to come up with a way to turn a "mess of taters" into an elegant presentation for my B&B guests, so of course, I turned to cast iron. Cast iron and a late morning campfire go together like a cup and coffee.

MAKES: 4 TRAYS

1. Preheat oven to 450°F. Lightly butter eight 9-oz cast-iron oval mini-servers.

2. Add potatoes to a large bowl. Melt 2 T butter and add to potatoes. Add salt and pepper and toss to coat. Evenly divide potatoes between two large baking sheets and spread in a single layer. Bake, turning frequently, until potatoes are golden brown and slightly crisp (about 35 minutes). Remove from oven and cool slightly.

3. Reduce oven temperature to 350°F.

4. In a small skillet, sauté garlic in remaining 4 T butter until golden brown. Remove from heat; stir in parsley. Set aside.

5. Arrange a layer of potatoes in the bottom of prepared oval mini-servers. Evenly divide Cheddar among trays and top each tray with 1 T Parmesan. Evenly divide remaining potatoes, Gruyère, and remaining Parmesan among trays. Evenly divide garlic/parsley mixture among trays; pour 2 T cream over each tray.

6. Place trays on a large baking sheet and bake for 25 minutes, or until cheese is golden brown.

Vintage Tabletop, Hand Crank, Cast-Iron Potato Slicer

&& Any chance I can get your recipe for the cast-iron potatoes you served to me and my husband when we stayed at your B&B this past summer? I can't get them off my mind. They were that good. **&&**

– Mildred "Milly" Ross

Enameled Cast-Iron Mini
Round Cocotte
(Note: this recipe calls for 6 cocottes)

⅔   cup sour cream
½   cup milk
¼   cup heavy cream
½   t salt
¾   lb yellow potatoes, sliced into
     ⅛"-thick slices
6   ozs sharp Cheddar cheese,
     shredded (about 1½ cups)
1   T minced chives

Sour Cream & Chive Single-Serve Scalloped Potatoes

Scalloped potatoes are always a favorite at the farm, so it's no surprise that we're always dreaming up new flavor combinations and serving methods. The straightforward prep of this recipe makes it a great choice when you're short on time but don't want to sacrifice flavor or flair.

MAKES: 6 SERVINGS

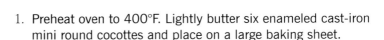

1. Preheat oven to 400°F. Lightly butter six enameled cast-iron mini round cocottes and place on a large baking sheet.

2. In a small bowl, whisk sour cream, milk, cream, and salt together.

3. In the bottom of each mini round cocotte, arrange layer of potatoes, overlapping each slice. Add about 1 T sour-cream mixture to each, and then add about 1 T cheese. Repeat once more.

4. For the top layer, evenly divide remaining potatoes, cheese, and sour cream mixture between cocottes. Bake for 45 minutes, or until potatoes are tender. Top with chives and serve.

5-qt Cast-Iron Dutch Oven

2½ lb yellow potatoes,
    sliced into ⅛"-thick slices
1   t salt, divided
1   t pepper, divided
4   ozs Parmesan cheese, shredded
    (about 1 cup), divided
2   cups heavy cream
2   ozs Cheddar cheese, shredded
    (about ½ cup)

gluten free

Tip: a mandoline slicer makes
quick work of slicing potatoes
to a uniform thickness.

DUTCH-OVEN SCALLOPED POTATOES

Who doesn't love a big mess of scalloped potatoes? With the help of a mandoline slicer, this recipe is a snap to prepare. I find the process of layering potatoes in tidy little rings around my Dutch oven cathartic. I love creating something that looks tidy and orderly and tastes good to boot.

MAKES: 8 SERVINGS

1. Preheat oven to 375°F. Lightly butter a 5-qt cast-iron Dutch oven.

2. Arrange potato slices in a single layer in the bottom of the Dutch oven. Sprinkle with about ¼ t salt and ¼ t pepper, then add ¼ cup grated Parmesan. Continue layering, ending with potatoes.

3. Pour cream over all and top with Cheddar.

4. Cover and bake for 45 minutes. Remove lid and bake an additional 15–20 minutes until top is golden and potatoes are tender.

VINTAGE CAST IRON

While my modern cast-iron Dutch oven at left sports two side-mounted handles, my vintage model above also features a heavy hanger, perfect for hanging over the campfire. In days of old, these hangers often suspended a pot of simmering stew or hearty soup over an open kitchen fireplace fueled by wood.

What do you get when you have a plateful of "biscuit buns" and a skillet full of yummy, cheesy, spiced-up burger? DINNER FOR 4.

What do you get when you bake up a whole lotta "biscuit buns" and then make all eight of my slider recipes? BUFFET FOR 32!

For six of the recipes, you simply combine the ingredients and "burger binder" in a bowl, mix, and then bake. For busy families without time to fuss and flip burgers, this menu is perfect. For entertaining guests, these sliders make serving a variety of delicious foods a snap.

BISCUIT BUNS & BURGER BINDER

MAKES: 16 BISCUIT BUNS (4 SERVINGS)

2½ cups flour, plus more for dusting
2½ t cream of tartar
1½ t baking soda
1½ t salt
5 T cold butter
1¼ cups buttermilk

9" Cast-Iron Skillet

14" Cast-Iron Baking Pan

1. Preheat oven to 450°F.

BURGER BINDER

2. In a large bowl, combine flour, cream of tartar, baking soda, and salt. Pull out ½ cup of the dry ingredients for the "burger binder" used in our slider recipes.

3. Using a pastry blender or fork, cut butter into dry ingredients until mixture resembles coarse crumbs with some pea-size chunks throughout.

4. Make a depression in the center of the mix to receive the liquid. Add buttermilk all at once and mix just enough to form a sticky dough (do not overmix).

5. Turn the dough out onto a generously floured work surface and press out to about ¼"-³⁄₈" thickness. Dip a 2" cookie cutter in flour and cut out 32 biscuits. On a 14" cast-iron baking pan, stack two biscuits, one on top of the other, to create "biscuit buns" so that you have 16 double buns.

6. Bake for 8–10 minutes, or until tops are light golden brown.

The key to perfect biscuits is to start with a wet, sticky dough that you've barely mixed.

Create a soft pillow of flour on your cutting board, and using generously floured hands, transfer the dough from your bowl.

Remember, the key to perfect biscuits is to work your dough as little as possible.

Gently press dough to ¼"–⅜" thickness. No rolling pin needed!

Cut 32 biscuits using a 2" biscuit cutter, then stack one on top of another to create "biscuit buns" that stick together after baking, but separate easily.

Onion & Swiss Sliders:

3	T olive oil
1	yellow onion, peeled and sliced into half-rings
1	lb lean ground beef
½	t salt
½	t pepper
	Burger Binder, p. 74
8	ozs Swiss cheese, shredded (about 1 cup)

Taco Sliders:

1	lb lean ground beef
½	medium onion, peeled and diced (about 1 cup)
1	garlic clove, peeled and minced (about 1 t)
½	t crushed red pepper flakes
½	t salt
½	t pepper
	Burger Binder, p. 74
1	cup refried beans
8	ozs Cheddar cheese, shredded (about 1 cup)
1	tomato, finely diced (about ¾ cup)
1	avocado, finely diced (about ½ cup)
½	cup sour cream

CARAMELIZED ONION & SWISS SLIDERS

MAKES: 16 SLIDERS

1. Preheat oven to 375°F.

2. Preheat oil in a large skillet over medium-low heat; add onion slices, stirring to coat evenly. Cover and cook 15 minutes, stirring occasionally. Remove cover; reduce heat to low. Continue cooking, stirring occasionally, until onion slices release their sugar and begin to caramelize and turn golden brown (about 30 minutes).

3. In a large bowl, combine beef, salt, pepper, onion slices, and binder; mix well.

4. Spoon mixture into a 9" cast-iron skillet. Bake for 25 minutes, sprinkle cheese evenly on top, and continue baking for 20 minutes.

TACO SLIDERS

MAKES: 16 SLIDERS

1. Preheat oven to 375°F.

2. In a large bowl, combine beef, onion, garlic, pepper flakes, salt, pepper, and binder; mix well.

3. Spoon mixture into a 9" cast-iron skillet. Spread beans evenly over the top. Bake for 25 minutes, sprinkle cheese evenly on top, and continue baking for 20 minutes. Serve with tomato, avocado, and sour cream.

EGGIE SLIDERS

MAKES: 16 SLIDERS

1. Preheat oven to 375°F.

2. In a large bowl, combine veggies, garlic, salt, pepper, and binder; mix well.

3. Spoon mixture into a 9" cast-iron skillet. Bake for 25 minutes, sprinkle cheese evenly on top, and continue baking for 20 minutes.

LOPPY-JOE SLIDERS

MAKES: 16 SLIDERS

1. Preheat oven to 375°F.

2. In a medium bowl, combine first five ingredients. Add water and tomato paste, mix well.

3. In a large bowl, combine beef, onion, bell pepper, garlic, and binder; add tomato-spice mixture and mix well.

4. Spoon mixture into a 9" cast-iron skillet. Bake for 45 minutes.

Veggie Sliders:

1	zucchini, diced (about 1½ cups)
1	carrot, diced (about 1 cup)
½	medium onion, peeled and diced (about 1 cup)
4	ozs mushrooms, diced (about 1 cup)
1	red bell pepper, seeded and finely diced (about 1¼ cups)
1	garlic clove, peeled and minced (about 1 t)
½	t salt
¼	t pepper

Burger Binder, p. 74

8	ozs manchego cheese, shredded (about 1 cup)

Sloppy-Joe Sliders:

1½	t chili powder
1	t salt
½	t pepper
¼	t cumin
1	t brown sugar
¼	cup water
1	6-oz can tomato paste
1	lb lean ground beef
½	onion, peeled and diced (about 1 cup)
1	green bell pepper, seeded and finely diced (about 1¼ cups)
2	garlic cloves, peeled and minced (about 2 t)

Burger Binder, p. 74

Mustard Topping

Cheese Topping

Smoked-Salmon Sliders:

2	8-oz smoked salmon fillets, skinned
¼	fennel bulb, trimmed and finely minced (about ¼ cup)
1	oz Gruyère cheese, shredded (about ¼ cup)
2	t Dijon mustard
1	t fresh dill, minced

Sausage & Gravy Sliders:

2	T butter
4	ozs mushrooms, sliced (about 1 cup)
¾	cup white wine
1	cup heavy cream
½	t salt
½	t pepper
1	lb spicy sausage
	Burger Binder, p. 74
8	ozs smoked Gouda cheese, shredded (about 1 cup)

Smoked-Salmon Sliders

MAKES: 16 SLIDERS

Note: Each fillet has a different topping.

1. Preheat oven to 375°F.

2. Place salmon fillets in a 14" cast-iron baking pan.

3. Cover one fillet with fennel and cheese. Cover second fillet with mustard and dill.

4. Bake for 15 minutes.

Spicy Sausage & Gravy Sliders

MAKES: 16 SLIDERS

1. Preheat oven to 375°F.

2. Melt butter in large skillet over medium heat; sauté mushrooms for 5 minutes, stirring occasionally. Reduce heat to medium-low, add wine, and simmer for 15 minutes. Reduce heat to low, add cream, and continue cooking for 10 minutes. Stir in salt and pepper; remove from heat. Add sausage and binder; mix well, breaking up sausage into small, ½" chunks.

3. Spoon mixture into a 9" cast-iron skillet. Bake for 25 minutes, sprinkle cheese evenly on top, and continue baking for 20 minutes.

GARLIC & CHEDDAR SLIDERS

MAKES: 16 SLIDERS

1. Preheat oven to 375°F.

2. In a large bowl, combine beef, garlic, salt, pepper, and binder; mix well.

3. Spoon mixture into a 9" cast-iron skillet. Bake for 25 minutes, sprinkle cheese evenly on top, and continue baking for 20 minutes.

Garlic & Cheddar Sliders:

1	lb lean ground beef
4	garlic cloves, peeled and minced (about 4 t)
½	t salt
½	t pepper
Burger Binder, p. 74	
8	ozs Cheddar cheese, shredded (about 1 cup)

STEAK & BLUE-CHEESE SLIDERS

MAKES: 16 SLIDERS

1. Preheat oven to 375°F.

2. Melt butter in a large skillet over medium heat; sauté mushrooms for 10 minutes, stirring occasionally.

3. In a medium bowl, combine beef, binder, and pepper.

4. Place beef mixture in a 9" cast-iron skillet; cover evenly with mushrooms and cheese. Bake for 45 minutes.

Steak & Blue-Cheese Sliders:

2½	T butter
8	ozs mushrooms, sliced (about 2 cups)
2	8-oz New York strip steaks, trimmed and thinly sliced
Burger Binder, p. 74	
¼	t pepper
9	ozs blue cheese, crumbled (about 1 cup)

79

TORTILLAS

2 cups flour
¾ t salt
¾ t baking powder
½ cup coconut oil (in solid form)
¾ cup warm water

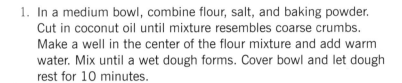

When my DIL, Ashley, and I set out to create this tortilla recipe, we had a few goals in mind. We wanted to create flavorful tortillas without hydrogenated oils or other strange ingredients. The texture was important as well. We didn't want a gummy tortilla, but rather one that you can feel your teeth sink into without it being tough or chewy. These tortillas are amazingly pliable, and the texture is just right—substantial and not too soft. Lastly, the coconut oil gives the tortillas a subtle coconut flavor that is out-of-this-world delicious.

MAKES: TWELVE 6½" TORTILLAS

10½" Cast-Iron Griddle

8" Cast-Iron Tortilla Press

1. In a medium bowl, combine flour, salt, and baking powder. Cut in coconut oil until mixture resembles coarse crumbs. Make a well in the center of the flour mixture and add warm water. Mix until a wet dough forms. Cover bowl and let dough rest for 10 minutes.

2. Over medium-low heat, preheat a 10½" cast-iron griddle.

3. Cut two 8½" squares of wax paper.

4. Divide dough into 12 equal portions. Form one portion into a ball. Press dough in 8" cast-iron tortilla press between squares of wax paper. Flip flattened dough over (in wax paper), and press again. Lift wax paper from dough, replace, and continue to press until dough holds its shape (it will want to shrink during the first few presses).

5. After pressing, carefully lift the wax paper, replace, and flip over. Continue doing this until the wax paper readily lifts from the tortilla. Remove one side of the wax paper and place tortilla on your hand. Carefully remove the other piece of wax paper. Transfer tortilla to preheated griddle.

6. Cook tortilla for 30–45 seconds, or until top of tortilla has lost its sheen. Flip over and cook for an additional 30–45 seconds. Transfer cooked tortilla to a cooling rack and repeat process with remaining dough (if griddle gets too hot during cooking and pressing, reduce heat or turn off intermittently).

7. Cool tortillas completely and transfer to an airtight container or Ziploc bag. Reheat just before serving.

8" Cast-Iron Skillet

Filling:

1	lb ground pork
4	ozs cabbage, finely shredded (about 1 cup)
6	shiitake mushrooms, finely diced (about ⅔ cup)
¼	oz chives, minced (about ¼ cup)
¼	cup fresh cilantro leaves, minced
2	garlic cloves, peeled and minced (about 2 t)
¼	t fresh grated ginger
½	t salt
¼	t white pepper

Wrappers:

1¼	cups flour
¼	t salt
2	egg whites
¼	cup water
3	T cornstarch
¼	cup safflower oil, divided

Dipping Sauce:

2	T soy sauce
1	T brown sugar
1	T mirin
1	t toasted sesame oil
⅛	t fresh grated ginger
mustard for serving	

FRIED POT STICKERS

Don't be intimidated by the appearance of these pot stickers—they're really quite simple to make. All it takes is mixing up a little meat and spices, and making the wrappers. After that, you're well on your way to shaping these cute little pouches and frying them up in your trusty cast-iron skillet.

MAKES: 32 POTSTICKERS

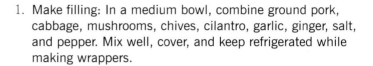

1. Make filling: In a medium bowl, combine ground pork, cabbage, mushrooms, chives, cilantro, garlic, ginger, salt, and pepper. Mix well, cover, and keep refrigerated while making wrappers.

2. Make wrappers: In a small bowl, combine flour and salt. In another small bowl, whisk egg whites and water together.

3. Make a depression in the center of the flour and pour in the egg-white mixture. Stir until a dough forms. Let dough rest for 10 minutes.

4. While dough is resting, prepare dipping sauce: In a small bowl, combine all ingredients and mix well. Cover and refrigerate.

5. Line two large baking sheets with wax paper.

6. Assemble pot stickers: Dust a clean work surface with cornstarch and roll dough out to an 18" square, dusting with cornstarch as needed. Using a 3"-round cookie cutter, cut dough into 32 circles.

7. Arrange circles on prepared cookie sheets. Spoon 1 T filling onto each circle. Fold each circle in half around the filling and crimp the edges to seal. Flatten bottom so pot stickers can stand up.

8. Add 2 T safflower oil to an 8" cast-iron skillet and heat over medium-low heat. Once oil is shimmering, begin frying pot stickers in batches, adding remaining oil as needed. First, fry on the bottom for 1½–2 minutes, and then on each side for 1½–2 minutes or until golden brown.

9. Serve with dipping sauce and mustard.

10¼" Cast-Iron Skillet

Sweet-Corn Casserole:

1½	cups fresh or thawed frozen corn, divided
2	eggs
½	cup butter, melted
¾	cup sour cream
½	cup sugar
1	t salt
1	4-oz can diced green chiles (can substitute ½ cup fresh poblano chile, finely diced)
3	ozs cooked ham, cut into ¼" cubes (about ½ cup)
1	cup cornmeal
⅔	cup white rice flour
1	T baking powder

Skillet Corn Bread

Skillet Corn Bread:

1	cup flour
1	cup finely ground cornmeal
½	t baking powder
½	t baking soda
½	t salt
1	cup buttermilk
1	egg
2	T honey
4	T butter, melted

 # SWEET-CORN CASSEROLE

This casserole is a definite crowd pleaser. It lands somewhere on the texture spectrum between spoon bread and corn bread—still sliceable, but incredibly tender and soft. It's so deceptively gluten-free that when you whip up a batch, you'll have people exclaiming, "I can't believe this is gluten-free!"

MAKES: 6 SERVINGS

1. Preheat oven to 350°F. Generously butter a 10¼" cast-iron skillet.

2. Combine 1 cup corn and eggs in a food processor; blend. Transfer to a large bowl. Add butter, sour cream, sugar, and salt; mix thoroughly. Add remaining ½ cup corn, green chiles, and ham; mix.

3. In another bowl, combine cornmeal, rice flour, and baking powder.

4. Combine wet and dry ingredients; stir until just blended.

5. Transfer mixture to prepared skillet. Bake for 50 minutes, or until casserole is puffed in center, golden brown around edges, and a toothpick inserted in the center comes out clean.

 # SKILLET CORN BREAD

You can't have a cast-iron book without a skillet corn-bread recipe. Hot and buttered, it's quintessential cast iron.

MAKES: 4 SERVINGS

1. Preheat oven to 400°F. Generously butter an 8" cast-iron skillet.

2. In a medium bowl, combine flour, cornmeal, baking powder, baking soda, and salt.

3. In another medium bowl, combine buttermilk, egg, and honey. Whisk in melted butter (butter will chill and make the mixture slightly lumpy).

4. Add buttermilk mixture to flour mixture and mix well. Spoon batter into prepared skillet.

5. Bake for 22–25 minutes, or until a toothpick inserted into the center comes out clean.

Sweet Corn Casserole

gluten free

 EALTHY CORN DOGGIES

1	cup flour
¾	cup cornmeal
⅓	cup sugar
2	t baking powder
¾	t salt
5	T cold butter
1	cup vegetables, steamed and puréed (we used beets for one batch, carrots for another, and kale for the third)
½	cup water (or cooking liquid from vegetables)
1	egg

1. Preheat oven to 425°F. Lightly butter a cast-iron cornstick pan.

2. In a medium bowl, combine flour, cornmeal, sugar, baking powder, and salt. Using a pastry blender or fork, cut butter into dry ingredients until mixture resembles coarse crumbs with some pea-sized pieces throughout.

3. In a small bowl, combine vegetables, water or cooking liquid, and egg; stir into dry ingredients and mix just until combined.

4. Spoon batter into prepared pan, filling each cornstick cavity to the top. Bake for 25 minutes, until tops begin to brown. Repeat with remaining batter.

MAKES: 14 CORN DOGGIES

Cast-Iron Cornstick Pan

85

Sweet Corn Casserole

SECTION 3

BREADS & SOUPS

This photo of my neighbor's barn deserved more than the usual print-then-frame treatment. Instead, I had it printed onto a 14" square framed, stretched canvas (essentially an oversized embroidery hoop), and then embellished sections of it with embroidered French knots. This photo of it doesn't do it justice. When you see it in person on the wall, the embroidery gives it a three-dimensional feel and a rich texture that is stunning. If you're new to embroidery, this is a good beginner project. When first embarking on embroidery, an "even-weave" fabric is often used to learn the techniques of different stitches because its square weave makes it easy to put the needle right where you want it. A printed canvas has this same square weave, plus you get a "pattern" picture to go by.

14" Cast-Iron Baking Pan

BUTTERMILK BISCUITS

Tender, flaky, and moist buttermilk biscuits make the perfect accompaniment to soups and stews—or enjoy them as a stand-alone snack. If you have 25 minutes to spare, I strongly encourage you to get out your baking gear and get cookin'—you can thank me later.

HALF BATCH MAKES: SIX 3" BISCUITS
FULL BATCH MAKES: TWELVE 3" BISCUITS

Half Batch:

2	cups flour, plus more for dusting
1	T baking powder
¼	t baking soda
¼	t salt
¼	cup cold butter
1	cup buttermilk

Full Batch:

4	cups flour, plus more for dusting
2	T baking powder
½	t baking soda
½	t salt
½	cup cold butter
2	cups buttermilk

1. Preheat oven to 450°F.

2. In a large bowl, combine flour, baking powder, baking soda, and salt.

3. Using a pastry blender or fork, cut butter into dry ingredients until mixture resembles coarse crumbs with some pea-sized pieces throughout.

4. Make a depression in the center of the mix to receive the liquid. Add buttermilk all at once and mix just until dough forms (do not overmix).

5. Dust a clean work surface with flour and roll out to 1" thickness. Dip a 3" cookie cutter in flour and cut out biscuits (cut 6 biscuits if making recipe for a half batch, and 12 biscuits if making recipe for a full batch). Arrange biscuits ½" apart on a 14" cast-iron baking pan.

6. Bake for 10–12 minutes, or until tops are light golden brown.

Victorian Cast-Iron Cookbook Stand

It's the little things, isn't it, when it comes to your kitchen counter? This gem completes my kitchen. It sits on my counter next to my cast-iron cow paper-towel dispenser. Next to my cow sits a little cast-iron songbird that holds a roll of bath tissue. For my brand of cookbooks (including this one), my little stand works because mine are bound using something called a "lay-flat" binding. Why fight a cookbook? It needs to lay flat … in my book. Pretty as you please, my little Victorian-style cast-iron stand is available from EsschertDesignUSA.com.

15" x 12¼" Cast-Iron Rectangular Griddle

Sprouted Grain Biscuits:

2	cups sprouted whole-wheat flour, plus more for dusting
2	t baking powder
¾	t salt
½	t baking soda
6	T cold butter, cut into pieces
1½	cups buttermilk

Vintage Cast-Iron Cherry Pitter

Cherry-Pie Freezer Jam:

3	lbs fresh or thawed frozen pie cherries (about 8 cups), stemmed and pitted
2	cups sugar
¾	t MaryJane's ChillOver Powder
1½	T fresh lemon juice
2	t almond extract

MaryJane's
ChillOver Powder,
MaryJanesFarm.org

Sprouted-Grain Buttermilk Biscuits

Have you tried sprouted-grain flour yet? It's an ingredient with a bit of buzz surrounding it. The idea is that sprouted grain is easier to digest than its conventional cousin. That sounds great, but what I like most about sprouted grain is its hearty, sweet, earthy flavor.

MAKES: 12 BISCUITS

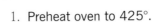

1. Preheat oven to 425°.

2. In a medium bowl, combine flour, baking powder, salt, and baking soda.

3. Using a pastry blender or fork, cut butter into dry ingredients until mixture resembles coarse crumbs with some pea-sized pieces throughout.

4. Make a depression in the center of the mix to receive the liquid. Add buttermilk all at once and mix just until dough forms (do not overmix).

5. Dust a clean work surface with flour and roll out to ½" thickness. Dip a 3" cookie cutter in flour and cut out biscuits. Arrange biscuits ½" apart on a 15" x 12¼" cast-iron griddle.

6. Bake for 15 minutes, or until tops are golden brown.

Cherry-Pie Freezer Jam

Is there anything more cheery than cherry-pie jam? Every year, the picking of cherries from our trees falls to my daughter so she can make our first cherry pie of the season. After that, we put up her favorite preserves, cherry-pie jam.

MAKES: 7 CUPS

1. Add pitted cherries to a large saucepan. Using an immersion blender, coarsely blend cherries (or use a food processor and pulse until coarsely diced).

2. Add sugar and mix well. Bring to a simmer over medium heat. Sprinkle in ChillOver Powder and simmer for an additional 3 minutes. Stir in lemon juice and almond extract.

3. Transfer jam to assorted canning jars (leave about ½" of space at the tops for expansion), or cool and transfer to airtight freezer containers. For immediate use, chill jam until set. Otherwise, freeze.

Cast-Iron Breadstick Pan

BREADSTICKS

When I think of these breadsticks, one word comes to mind: Crust. The curved bottom of my cast-iron breadstick pan hugs each breadstick, creating a wonderfully crisp crust. It takes measured self-control not to eat the whole pan.

MAKES: 11 BREADSTICKS

¾   cup warm water
2   T olive oil
1   t honey
1   package active dry yeast
    (about 2¼ t)
1¾ cups flour, plus more for dusting
¼   cup semolina flour
½   t salt
1   T Italian seasoning
1   oz Cheddar cheese, shredded
    (about ¼ cup)

1. In a small bowl, combine warm water, olive oil, and honey; whisk until honey is dissolved (mixture shouldn't feel hot on the inside of your wrist). Whisk in yeast and set aside.

2. Add flour, semolina flour, and salt to a stand mixer fitted with a dough hook. Make a depression in the center of the flour to receive the liquid; add yeast mixture to flour.

3. Mix until dough forms, and continue to mix until dough is smooth and pliable (5–8 minutes).

4. Lightly oil a medium bowl with olive oil. Dust hands and dough with flour and shape dough into a ball. Place in prepared bowl, cover with plastic wrap, and let rise in a warm place for 1½ hours, or until doubled in bulk.

5. Preheat oven to 425°F. Generously butter cavities in a cast-iron breadstick pan.

6. Deflate dough and divide into 11 portions. Roll each portion into a 7"-long rope and place in breadstick pan.

7. Sprinkle each breadstick with Italian seasoning and cheese. Bake for 12–14 minutes, or until golden brown.

CHEESESTICKS

If you're feeling a little cheesy, try whipping up a batch of these cheesesticks. I love the addition of grated Parmesan cheese to the dough. While you're at it, cook up a batch of my Red-Pepper Marinara (p. 94) for dipping.

MAKES: 11 CHEESESTICKS

1. In a small bowl, combine warm water, olive oil, and honey; whisk until honey is dissolved (mixture shouldn't feel hot on the inside of your wrist). Whisk in yeast and set aside.

2. Add flour, semolina flour, Parmesan cheese, and salt to a stand mixer fitted with a dough hook. Make a depression in the center of the flour to receive the liquid; add yeast mixture to flour.

3. Mix until dough forms, and continue to mix until dough is smooth and pliable (5–8 minutes).

4. Lightly oil a medium bowl with olive oil. Dust hands and dough with flour and shape dough into a ball. Place in prepared bowl, cover with plastic wrap, and let rise in a warm place for 1½ hours, or until doubled in bulk.

5. Preheat oven to 425°F. Generously butter cavities in a cast-iron breadstick pan.

6. Deflate dough and divide into 11 portions. Roll each portion into a 7"-long rope and place in breadstick pan.

7. Sprinkle each cheesestick with Gruyère and Asiago cheeses. Bake for 12–14 minutes, or until golden brown.

Cast-Iron Breadstick Pan

¾ cup warm water
2 T olive oil
1 t honey
1 package active dry yeast (about 2¼ t)
1½ cups flour, plus more for dusting
¼ cup semolina flour
1 oz Parmesan cheese, grated (about ¼ cup)
½ t salt
1 oz Gruyère cheese, shredded (about ¼ cup)
1 oz Asiago cheese, shredded (about ¼ cup)

Red-Pepper Marinara, p. 94

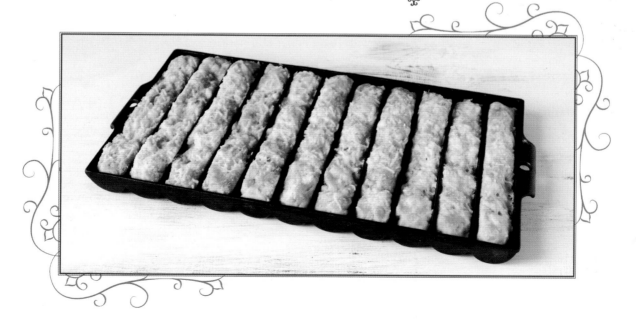

36-oz Cast-Iron Oval Serving Dish

Monkey Bread:

1¼	cups lukewarm water
1	t sugar
1	package active dry yeast (about 2¼ t)
3½	cups flour, plus more for dusting
¾	cup chives, minced
¼	cup parsley, minced
2	garlic cloves, peeled and minced (about 2 t)
½	t salt
4	T butter, melted
1	oz grated Parmesan cheese (about ⅓ cup)

Red-Pepper Marinara:

1	15-oz can crushed tomatoes
¼	cup red wine
2	garlic cloves, peeled and minced (about 2 t)
1	red bell pepper, seeded and diced (about 1¼ cups)
½	t honey
½	t salt
¼	t pepper

Herb & Parmesan Monkey Bread

Already broken up into bite-sized pieces, this monkey bread is ready-made for dipping and sharing. So go ahead, dig in, but no double-dipping, please!

MAKES: 6 SERVINGS

1. In a small bowl, combine water, sugar, and yeast. Set aside for about 5 minutes, or until frothy.

2. In a stand mixer fitted with a dough hook, combine flour, chives, parsley, garlic, and salt. Make a depression in the center of the flour to receive the liquid.

3. Add yeast mixture to flour mixture. Mix until dough forms and continue mixing until dough is smooth and pliable (about 5–8 minutes).

4. Lightly butter a medium bowl, form the dough into a ball, and place in the bowl. Lightly butter top of dough and cover with plastic wrap. Let dough rise in a warm place until it has doubled in bulk (about 1½ hours).

5. Preheat oven to 350°F. Lightly butter a 36-oz cast-iron oval serving dish.

6. Deflate dough and flatten to ½" thickness. Brush with butter and cut into ½" cubes. Add cubes to a medium bowl along with butter and Parmesan; toss to combine.

7. Transfer cubes to prepared oval server, cover with plastic wrap, and let rise in warm place for 30 minutes.

8. Remove plastic wrap and bake for 30–35 minutes. Serve with Red Pepper Marinara.

Red-Pepper Marinara

MAKES: 1½ CUPS

1. In a medium saucepan, combine all ingredients. Bring to a simmer over medium heat, reduce heat to low, and simmer until wine is reduced and sauce is thickened, stirring occasionally.

12" Cast-Iron Skillet

¼   cup warm water
1   package active dry yeast
     (about 2¼ t)
1   t sugar
4   cups flour, plus more for dusting
¾   cup buttermilk
6   T butter, divided
¼   cup brown sugar
1   t salt
1   sweet potato, peeled
     and cooked
1   egg

Sweet-Potato Rolls

I love the subtle orange hue of these sweet-potato rolls. They nestle right into my 12" cast-iron skillet, and once baked, lift right out. They're divine warm with a generous smear of butter.

MAKES: 12 ROLLS

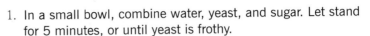

1. In a small bowl, combine water, yeast, and sugar. Let stand for 5 minutes, or until yeast is frothy.

2. Meanwhile, add flour to a stand mixer fitted with a dough hook. Make a depression in the center of the flour to receive the liquid; set aside.

3. In a small saucepan, combine buttermilk, 4 T butter, brown sugar, and salt. Cook over low heat, stirring frequently until sugar is dissolved and butter begins to melt. Mixture shouldn't feel hot on the inside of your wrist.

4. Add sweet potato to a food processor; pour in milk mixture and egg. Pulse until mixture is smooth.

5. Add yeast and milk mixture to the flour. Mix until dough forms and continue mixing until dough is smooth and pliable (about 5–8 minutes).

6. Lightly butter a medium bowl. Dust hands and dough with flour and shape into a ball. Place in prepared bowl, cover with plastic wrap, and let rise in a warm place for 1½ hours, or until doubled in bulk.

7. Preheat oven to 350°F.

8. In a 12" cast-iron skillet over low heat, melt 1 T butter. Remove from heat and brush melted butter all over bottom and sides of skillet; set aside.

9. Deflate dough and divide it into 12 equal portions. Shape into balls, and arrange in skillet. Brush tops of rolls with remaining 1 T butter and cover with plastic wrap.

10. Let rolls rise for 20 minutes, remove plastic wrap, and bake for 20–25 minutes, or until tops are lightly browned.

Cast-Iron Loaf Pan

1¼   cups milk
1   T honey
1   T butter, cut into pieces
½   t salt
1   package active dry yeast
      (about 2¼ t)
3   cups flour, plus more for dusting
1   egg

I-MIGHT-DIE-TOMORROW WHITE BREAD

My white-bread-lovin' father-in-law, a farmer all his life, lived to age 98. His secret to longevity? Daily bacon (two strips), white-bread toast, and one egg (never two) poached in bacon grease.

MAKES: 1 LOAF

1. In a small saucepan, combine milk, honey, butter, and salt. Over medium-low heat, whisk mixture until honey is dissolved and butter begins to melt (mixture shouldn't feel hot on the inside of your wrist). Remove from heat, whisk in yeast, and set aside.

2. Add flour to a stand mixer fitted with a dough hook. Make a depression in the center of the flour to receive the liquid; add milk mixture and egg to flour.

3. Mix until dough forms, and continue to mix until dough is smooth and pliable (5–8 minutes).

4. Lightly butter a medium bowl. Dust hands and dough with flour and shape into a ball. Place in prepared bowl, cover with plastic wrap, and let rise in a warm place for 1½ hours, or until doubled in bulk.

5. Preheat oven to 350°F. Generously butter a cast-iron loaf pan.

6. Deflate dough (at this point, you can pinch off some of the dough and make Fried Scones, p. 99). On a lightly floured surface, gently press dough out into an 8½" x 10" rectangle. Beginning from an 8½" side, roll dough up, jelly-roll style. Pinch seams together at the bottom and sides.

7. Place dough into prepared loaf pan. Cover with plastic wrap and let rise for 30 minutes.

8. After 30 minutes, remove plastic wrap. Using a sharp knife, make a ⅛"-deep slash down the length of the loaf. Bake for 35–40 minutes, or until internal temperature reaches 200–205°F. Remove loaf from oven, brush top with butter, and transfer to a cooling rack to cool completely.

MOMMA BUTTERS' FRIED SCONES

My mother baked bread every week without fail for 50 years. One of my treats on bake day was a handful of dough she'd grab from the bowl, stretch and flatten with her hands, and then toss into a layer of hot butter she'd melted in her faithful cast-iron skillet. Onto a plate it would go so I could drench its crispy-yet-soft warmth in honey.

MAKES: 1 SERVING

8" Cast-Iron Skillet

Cast iron: mere child's play.

Cast-Iron Loaf Pan

CARROT BREAD

Moist, subtly sweet, with just the right amount of spice, this carrot bread will keep you coming back for more. For added decadence, slather it with cream-cheese frosting and sprinkle with walnuts. Yum!

MAKES: ONE LOAF

Carrot Bread:

1½   cups flour
1   t baking powder
1   t baking soda
¼   t salt
1   t cinnamon
½   t ground ginger
¼   t nutmeg
½   cup finely shredded coconut
½   cup walnuts, finely chopped
2   eggs, separated
4   T butter, softened
½   cup brown sugar
1   carrot, shredded (about 1 cup)
½   cup unsweetened applesauce
½   cup crushed pineapple

Cream-Cheese Frosting:

6   ozs cream cheese, softened
      (about ¾ cup)
3   T butter, softened
1½   t vanilla extract
1½   cups powdered sugar
¼   cup walnuts, finely chopped
      (optional)

1. Preheat oven to 350°F. Generously butter a cast-iron loaf pan.

2. In a medium bowl, combine flour, baking powder, baking soda, salt, cinnamon, ginger, nutmeg, coconut, and walnuts; set aside.

3. In a small bowl, whip egg whites into soft peaks; set aside.

4. In a medium bowl or stand mixer, combine egg yolks, butter, and brown sugar; whip until smooth. Add shredded carrot, applesauce, and pineapple; mix well.

5. Add flour mixture to carrot mixture and mix until smooth. Gently fold in egg whites.

6. Spoon batter into prepared loaf pan. Bake for 55–60 minutes, or until a toothpick inserted into the center comes out clean.

7. Remove bread from pan and cool on a wire rack.

8. Make frosting: In a medium bowl, combine cream cheese, butter, and vanilla. Mix with an electric mixer until smooth. Gradually mix in powdered sugar.

9. Frost carrot bread and sprinkle with finely chopped walnuts, if desired.

CARROT MUFFINS WITH CREAM-CHEESE FILLING

If you're gluten-free, these muffins are proof that you can still have your cake (well, muffin) and eat it, too. While the muffins themselves are delicious, I'm partial to their cream-cheese centers.

MAKES: 6 MUFFINS

6-Cavity Cast-Iron Muffin Pan

1. Preheat oven to 350°F. Line a 6-cavity cast-iron muffin pan with paper liners.

2. Make filling: Combine cream cheese, powdered sugar, and vanilla in a small bowl and mix until smooth. Set aside.

3. Make muffins: In a small bowl, combine white rice flour, tapioca flour, baking powder, baking soda, salt, raisins, cinnamon, ginger, and nutmeg; set aside.

4. In another small bowl, whip egg white into soft peaks; set aside.

5. In a medium bowl or stand mixer, combine egg yolk, butter, brown sugar, and honey; whip until smooth. Add shredded carrots, applesauce, and pineapple and mix well.

6. Add flour mixture to carrot mixture and mix until smooth. Gently fold in egg white.

7. Scoop about 1 T batter into each muffin cup. Make a slight indentation in center of batter with the back of a spoon and evenly divide cream-cheese filling among muffin cups. Evenly divide remaining muffin batter among cups. Bake for 25 minutes, or until a toothpick inserted into the center of a muffin comes out clean.

Cream-Cheese Filling:

2	ozs cream cheese (about ¼ cup), softened
1	T powdered sugar
¼	t vanilla

Carrot Muffins:

½	cup white rice flour
¼	cup tapioca flour
½	t baking powder
¼	t baking soda
¼	t salt
2	T raisins
½	t cinnamon
¼	t ground ginger
⅛	t ground nutmeg
1	egg, separated
2	T butter, softened
1	T brown sugar
1	T honey
¼	cup shredded carrots
¼	cup unsweetened applesauce
¼	cup crushed pineapple

gluten free

5-qt Cast-Iron Dutch Oven

Dumplings:

Half batch Buttermilk Biscuits p. 88

Creamy Chicken Soup:

1	T safflower oil
1½	lbs boneless, skinless chicken breasts
2	T butter
1	onion, peeled and finely diced (about 2 cups)
6	garlic cloves, peeled and minced (about 2 T)
1	carrot, peeled and diced (about 1 cup)
3	celery stalks, diced (about ¾ cup)
6	cups chicken broth
½	cup flour
⅔	cup water
1	cup sour cream
¼	cup fresh parsley, minced, plus more for garnish
1	t fresh thyme leaves
¼	t dried rosemary
¼	t celery seed
1	cup fresh or thawed frozen peas

 CHICKEN & "DUMPLINGS"

I know that chicken and dumplings are supposed to be as comforting as home and apple pie, but I've struggled to fall in love with the density of a dumpling. Maybe it's the size when trying to break one up enough to meld its flavor with a bit of creamy chicken in every bite. The solution? Cut the dumplings up first!

MAKES: 8 SERVINGS

1. In a medium skillet over medium heat, heat safflower oil. Once oil is hot, add chicken breasts and cook on each side for 6 minutes. Cover and cook an additional 6–8 minutes, or until internal temperature reaches 165°F. Remove chicken from pan and set aside to cool.

2. Meanwhile, in a 5-qt Dutch oven over medium heat, combine butter, onion, and garlic. Cook until onion is soft, stirring occasionally.

3. Add carrot, celery, and chicken broth. Bring to a simmer over medium heat; reduce heat to low.

4. Add flour and water to a 1-qt canning jar, attach lid, and shake vigorously until mixture is smooth. Pour flour paste into simmering chicken broth in a slow, steady stream, whisking constantly.

5. Once chicken broth is thickened, stir in sour cream, parsley, thyme, rosemary, and celery seed.

6. Using two forks, shred chicken and add to soup. Stir in peas. Continue to simmer over low heat.

7. Make Biscuit Dumplings: Prepare a half batch of biscuit dough according to instructions on p. 88. On a lightly floured surface, roll dough into an 8" x 18" rectangle. Cut dough into twenty-four ¾" x 8" strips. Cut each strip in half to make forty-eight ¾" x 4" strips.

8. Add biscuit strips to soup, stirring occasionally to disperse strips throughout soup.

9. Cover Dutch oven and continue to simmer over low heat for 40 minutes, or until biscuit strips are cooked, stirring halfway though.

10. Serve immediately. If desired, garnish with fresh parsley.

HAM & LIMA-BEAN SOUP

This was one of my mother's signature meals. It was our job to sort the beans on a counter (back then, there wasn't any shortage of dirt clods and rocks in a bag of lima beans). Salty ham and peppery beans in a broth? What's not to love?

MAKES: 8 SERVINGS

5-qt Cast-Iron Dutch Oven

1	lb dry lima beans (about 2½ cups), rinsed and soaked overnight
2	T butter
1	onion, peeled and minced (about 2 cups)
4	garlic cloves, peeled and minced (about 4 t)
6	cups chicken broth
2	fresh bay leaves
1	t fresh thyme
1	lb cooked ham, shredded (about 2⅔ cups)
2	T fresh parsley, minced

salt and pepper to taste

gluten free

1. Rinse and drain lima beans; set aside.

2. Melt butter in a 5-qt cast-iron Dutch oven over medium heat. Add onion and garlic; cook until tender, stirring occasionally.

3. Add lima beans, chicken broth, bay leaves, and thyme. Bring to a simmer, reduce heat to low, cover, and continue to cook for 3 hours, stirring occasionally.

4. After 3 hours, add ham and continue to cook on low 1½–2 hours, or until lima beans are tender.

5. Just before serving, remove and discard bay leaves and mix in parsley. Season with salt and pepper to taste.

5-qt Cast-Iron Dutch Oven

EARTY MEATBALL SOUP

A batch of soup happily simmering on the stove brings me great comfort. As the air fills with the rich aroma of this soup, it strengthens my view that there's nothing better than a home-cooked meal.

MAKES: 8 SERVINGS

Soup:

2	T olive oil
2	carrots, diced (about 2 cups)
1	red bell pepper, seeded and diced (about 1¼ cups)
2	celery stalks, halved lengthwise and sliced (about 1 cup)
½	onion, peeled and minced (about 1 cup), divided
4	garlic cloves, peeled and minced (about 4 t), divided
8	cups chicken broth
1	14½-oz can diced tomatoes
1½	lbs sweet potatoes, peeled and diced into ½" cubes (about 4½ cups)
1	cup orzo

Meatballs:

½	lb ground beef
½	lb Italian sausage
½	cup breadcrumbs
2	eggs
2	ozs Asiago cheese, shredded (about ½ cup), plus more for serving
¼	cup fresh parsley, minced
½	t salt
½	t pepper
¼	t baking soda
½	lb kale, stemmed and coarsely diced (about 8 cups)

1. Make soup: In a 5-qt cast-iron Dutch oven, combine oil, carrots, bell pepper, celery, ½ cup onion, and 2 t garlic. Cook over medium heat until onion is soft (7–9 minutes).

2. Add chicken broth, diced tomatoes, sweet potatoes, and orzo. Bring to a simmer and cook until sweet potatoes and orzo are tender, stirring occasionally.

3. Meanwhile, make meatballs: In a medium bowl, combine ground beef, sausage, breadcrumbs, eggs, Asiago, parsley, salt, pepper, baking soda, and remaining onion and garlic. Mix well and form mixture into 24 meatballs.

4. Once soup is simmering and sweet potatoes are tender, add meatballs and cook for an additional 15 minutes, or until internal temperature of meatballs reaches 160°F. Add kale and cook just until softened. If desired, serve with shredded Asiago.

5-qt Cast-Iron Dutch Oven

OLD-FASHIONED CHICKEN NOODLE SOUP

It's no wonder chicken noodle soup has become synonymous with healing and renewal. So much more than a mere soup, chicken noodle soup is in a class of its own, for good reason. Sometimes, it's the only food that sounds good.

MAKES: 8 SERVINGS

Pasta:

²⁄₃	cup flour
¹⁄₃	cup semolina flour
2	eggs
1	t olive oil

Soup:

1	half chicken (about 2 lbs)
1½	t olive oil
1¾	t salt, divided
1¼	t pepper, divided
1	bunch celery, sliced (about 4 cups)
4	carrots, quartered and sliced (about 4 cups)
1	onion, peeled and minced (about 2 cups)
4	garlic cloves, peeled and minced (about 4 t)
6	cups chicken broth

1. Make pasta: In a medium bowl, combine flours. Make a depression in the center, add eggs and olive oil, and gently mix with a fork. When the mixture is mostly large crumbs, transfer to a clean work surface and knead for 8–10 minutes, dusting with flour as needed. Shape dough into a disc, wrap in plastic wrap, and refrigerate for at least 2 hours.

2. Preheat oven to 400°F.

3. Make soup: Place chicken in a 5-qt Dutch oven, cavity side down. Rub chicken with olive oil, ¼ t salt, and ¼ t pepper. Cover and bake for 45 minutes, or until internal temperature reaches 165°F.

4. Remove chicken from Dutch oven and place on a cutting board to cool, leaving cooking juices in Dutch oven.

5. Add celery, carrots, onion, and garlic to Dutch oven and cook over medium heat for 10 minutes, until tender-crisp. Add chicken broth and remaining 1½ salt and 1 t pepper. Cook for 30 minutes, or until vegetables are tender.

6. Meanwhile, remove meat from chicken, breaking up into pieces; add to Dutch oven.

7. On a lightly floured surface, roll pasta out thin (if using a pasta maker, roll to a setting of 5) and cut into ½" x 2½" strips. Add noodles to soup and cook for 3–5 minutes.

Chicken Soup
for the Soul
... and mashed potatoes!

This photo is a surprise for my brother, Scott. When we were growing up, meals were less complex than they are today. For our family, a meal meant eating meat we'd raised ourselves (chicken or rabbit), fish we'd caught, or a deer we'd shot. Winter meals always included a "keeper" crop we'd grown (potatoes, carrots, beets, squash, or onions). For birthdays, the Butters' five children were allowed to choose a meal. My brother always chose mashed potatoes (full of butter and cream) with a ladle full of Mom's chicken noodle soup in the center. You start out eating this meal with a fork, but once the broth from the soup is no longer contained within the well of mashed potatoes, it's time for your soup spoon. After that, the mix of soup-y potatoes is mopped up with a piece of homemade buttered bread. By today's standards, this is way too much starch, but this meal defines comfort food. Scott, next time you visit, I know what you'll be requesting. I ate this entire plateful in your honor!

FRENCH ONION SOUP WITH CROÛTES

I love the way my Dutch oven perfectly caramelizes onions every time, making a superb base for this soup. Add crusty croûtes and melty Gruyère cheese, and you have a meal that's tough to top.

MAKES: 8 SERVINGS

Soup:

3	lbs onions (about 4 onions), peeled, halved lengthwise and thinly sliced
6	T butter
3	bay leaves
2	sprigs thyme
¼	cup flour
1	cup white wine
2	cups beef broth
2	cups chicken broth
1	t salt

Croûtes:

16	½"-thick diagonal slices of baguette
3	T butter, melted
6	oz Gruyère cheese, sliced

1. In a 5-qt Dutch oven, combine onions, butter, bay leaves, and thyme. Cook over medium heat for 1¼ hours, stirring occasionally. During cooking, onions will caramelize and turn a deep golden brown.

2. While onions are caramelizing, prepare croûtes. Preheat oven to 350°F. Arrange baguette slices on a 15" x 12¼" cast-iron griddle in a single layer and brush with melted butter. Bake for 20–25 minutes, or until crispy. Set aside.

3. Once onions are caramelized, stir in flour and cook for 1–2 minutes. Stir in wine and cook for 2 minutes. Add beef broth, chicken broth, and salt and bring to a simmer. Reduce heat to low and simmer for 30 minutes. Remove bay leaves and thyme sprigs.

4. To serve, divide soup between eight 10–12-oz soup crocks or oven-safe bowls, add two croûtes to each bowl, top with cheese, and broil for 3–5 minutes, until cheese is melted and bubbling.

5-qt Cast-Iron Dutch Oven

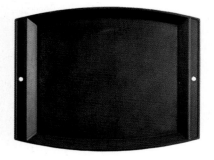

15" x 12¼" Cast-Iron Rectangular Griddle

10½" Cast-Iron Griddle

Crepes:

2   eggs
1   cup milk
¼   t salt
2   T butter, melted
1   cup flour, sifted

Make it gluten free: Substitute either white rice flour or almond meal/flour.

Filling:

2   T sugar
½   cup heavy cream
1   cup peanut butter or almond butter
1   cup peanuts or almonds, chopped
3   bananas, sliced

Spinach Artichoke Filling:

1   14-oz can artichoke hearts (not marinated), drained
4   cups fresh baby spinach
1   clove garlic
½   t salt
4   oz cream cheese, softened
1   cup Parmesan cheese, finely grated

COMFORT CREPES

Don't worry about getting super-thin crepes. To that end, you don't need a special crepe pan. My well-seasoned cast-iron griddle makes crepes that I'm proud to take to any potluck. I love crepes because they're so versatile. They're good for both desserts and savory dishes.

MAKES: SIX 8" CREPES

1. In a large bowl, whisk together eggs, milk, and salt. Whisk in melted butter and combine well, then whisk in flour. Refrigerate for at least 1 hour or up to 12 hours.

2. Heat a lightly-oiled 10½" cast-iron griddle over medium heat, reduce heat to low.

3. Pour about ⅓ cup batter onto the griddle and quickly use the bottom of your measuring cup to spread out the batter. (Note: if making gluten-free, almond meal/flour won't spread out, so your crepes will be smaller.)

4. Cook until top loses its sheen and bottom is lightly browned, then flip with a super-thin spatula and cook second side until slightly browned.

COMFORT-CREPES FILLING

MAKES: FILLING FOR SIX 8" CREPES

1. In a small bowl, combine sugar and cream. Whip until soft peaks form.

2. Place peanut or almond butter in a separate bowl. Fold in whipped cream until soft and creamy.

3. Spread ⅓ cup mixture down the middle of 1 crepe. Top with nuts and banana slices. (Optional: drizzle with honey.) Roll up. Repeat for remaining crepes.

SPINACH ARTICHOKE FILLING

MAKES: FILLING FOR SIX 8" CREPES

1. In a food processor, blend first four ingredients until mixed but still slightly chunky. Add cheeses and blend just until incorporated.

2. Spread ⅓ cup mixture down the middle of 1 crepe. Roll up. Repeat for remaining crepes.

TIP: Pour about ⅓ cup batter onto the griddle and quickly use the bottom of your measuring cup to spread the batter.

TIP: As you cook your crepes, slide them into a folded piece of foil; the steam will keep the crepes pliable and moist.

> " I had **rather be** on my **farm** than be **emperor** of the **world**. "
> – George Washington

5-qt Cast-Iron Dutch Oven

3	lbs bone-in chuck roast
10	garlic cloves, peeled and halved lengthwise
¼	cup safflower oil, divided
1	onion, peeled and quartered
1	lb carrots, peeled and cut into 2" lengths
4	thyme sprigs
3	rosemary sprigs
2	fresh bay leaves
1½	t salt
5⅔	cups water, divided
1	cup dry red wine
2	lbs white potatoes
8	ozs crimini mushrooms
½	cup flour

Pot Roast

MAKES: 6 SERVINGS

1. Preheat oven to 350°F.

2. With the tip of a sharp knife, cut 20 pocket holes for garlic throughout roast. Stuff each hole with half a garlic clove.

3. In a 5-qt cast-iron Dutch oven, heat 2 T safflower oil over medium heat. Once oil is hot, add roast and sear on each side for 3–4 minutes.

4. Once all sides of the roast are seared, remove from Dutch oven and place on a plate to rest. Sear onion quarters in Dutch oven for 1 minute on each side. Remove onions from Dutch oven. Add carrots and sear for 1 minute, stir, and sear an additional minute. Remove carrots. Remove Dutch oven from heat.

5. Place roast back in Dutch oven. Arrange onions, carrots, thyme, rosemary, and bay leaves around roast. Sprinkle with salt and pour in 5 cups water and wine. Cover roast and bake for 1½ hours.

6. Once roast has been in oven for 1½ hours, heat remaining 2 T safflower oil in a large skillet over medium heat.

7. Cut potatoes in half and add facedown to skillet. Sear for 2 minutes, or until potatoes are golden brown; remove from heat.

8. Remove roast from oven and add potatoes to Dutch oven. Cover Dutch oven and bake an additional 2–2½ hours, or until roast is fork tender.

9. Once roast is tender, use a slotted spoon to remove potatoes, carrots, onions, and roast. Discard bay leaves, thyme, and rosemary. Skim any fat from pan liquids and discard. Place Dutch oven with remaining liquids on stovetop.

10. Make gravy: Bring pan liquids to a simmer over medium heat and add mushrooms. Cook 2–3 minutes, or until tender and remove mushrooms from pan with a slotted spoon.

11. Add flour and remaining ⅔ cup water to a 1-qt canning jar, attach lid, and shake vigorously until mixture is smooth. Pour flour paste into simmering pan liquids in a slow, steady stream, whisking constantly.

12. Once gravy has thickened, break pot roast apart and serve with potatoes, onions, carrots, mushrooms, and gravy.

A good, old-fashioned pot roast never fails to please. When I was raising children, our only source of heat was a large wood stove that I stoked with firewood several times per day. A few hours before dinner, I'd prep a pot roast and put it to simmer on the wood stove. After a few hours, I'd add the vegetables, eventually making gravy and serving up dinner. Like the smell of bread fresh from the oven, a bubbling pot roast makes a house a home.

5-qt Cast-Iron Dutch Oven

Coffee Chili:

2	T olive oil
1½	lbs lean ground beef
4	cloves garlic, peeled and minced (about 4 t)
2	medium onions, peeled and diced (about 4 cups)
2	bell peppers, seeded and diced (about 2½ cups)
¼	cup chili powder
1	T dried oregano
1	t salt
½	t black pepper
¼	t cayenne pepper
1½	t sweet paprika
½	t cinnamon
1½	cups strongly brewed coffee (if serving children, use decaf)
2	28-oz cans crushed tomatoes
2	15-oz cans black beans, rinsed and drained (about 3½ cups)
2	T honey
2	T red-wine vinegar
2	bay leaves
2	jalapeño peppers, seeded and finely minced (about ¼ cup)

gluten free

Coffee Pot Roast:

2	T olive oil
3	lbs boneless chuck roast
salt and pepper	
3	onions, peeled and quartered
3	cloves garlic, peeled and minced (about 1 T)
½	t allspice
2	bay leaves
2	cups strongly brewed coffee (if serving children, use decaf)

Coffee Chili

Coffee in chili? While it sounds a bit offbeat, the addition of coffee will add complexity and depth of flavor. Rest assured, this chili will not taste anything like your morning cup of coffee, and the coffee flavor is subdued, not dominating.

MAKES: 8 SERVINGS

1. Heat oil in a 5-qt cast-iron Dutch oven over medium heat. Add ground beef; break up, and cook for 5 minutes. Add garlic, onions, and peppers; cook until meat is no longer pink and onions are tender. Add spices and cook for 1 minute.

2. Stir in remaining ingredients and bring to a boil. Reduce heat and simmer for 1–1½ hours. Discard bay leaves.

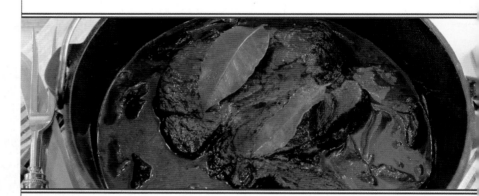

Coffee Pot Roast

As in the chili above, coffee adds a subtle flavor profile to a pot roast. In addition, the mild acidity of the coffee acts as a meat tenderizer, creating an irresistibly tender, melt-in-your-mouth roast.

MAKES: 8 SERVINGS

1. Heat oil in 5-qt lidded cast-iron Dutch oven. Place roast in pot, sprinkle generously with salt and pepper, and brown for several minutes on all sides. Add onions, garlic, and allspice around roast and cook for 5 minutes.

2. Place bay leaves on top of roast. Add coffee, bring to a boil, then reduce heat to a low simmer, cover, and cook for 3–4 hours, until roast is very tender. Discard bay leaves.

VINTAGE CAST IRON

This vintage coffee mill is both beautiful and practical. (But on the other hand, doesn't this describe all cast-iron gadgets?) Its gorgeous design makes it a beloved piece of kitchen décor, and its handy wooden drawer holds your ground coffee for that second pick-me-up pot.

12" Cast-Iron Skillet

12 ozs spaghetti
3   T butter, melted
3   ozs Parmesan cheese,
    shredded (about ¾ cup)
3   eggs, whisked
2   cups cottage cheese
3   cups spaghetti sauce
6   ozs mozzarella cheese,
    shredded (about 1½ cups)

SPAGHETTI PIE

Not only a lifesaver on those evenings you want to arrive home and make something easy, but filling, my Spaghetti Pie is also a hit at potlucks. Who wouldn't want a wedge of perfectly balanced spaghetti flavors in an easy-to-serve shape?

MAKES: 12 SERVINGS

1. Cook spaghetti according to package directions; drain, and toss with butter. Stir in Parmesan and eggs.

2. Preheat oven to 350°F.

3. Lightly butter a 12" cast-iron skillet. Spread spaghetti mixture on bottom, then a layer of cottage cheese, then a layer of spaghetti sauce. Top with mozzarella.

4. Bake uncovered for 40 minutes. Let sit for 5 minutes before serving.

EASY SKILLET LASAGNA

I've always regarded layered lasagnas as a large undertaking, so I wanted a shortcut version that still had all the elements and flavors of lasagna, but could be prepared in a fraction of the time. This skillet lasagna fits the bill.

MAKES: 12 SERVINGS

12" Cast-Iron Skillet

½	lb ground beef
½	lb Italian sausage
4	garlic cloves, peeled and minced (about 4 t)
3	15-oz cans tomato sauce
1	14.5-oz can diced tomatoes
1	t honey
1	t Italian seasoning
½	t pepper
¼	t dried basil
¼	t dried rosemary
8	ozs lasagna noodles, broken into pieces
6	ozs ricotta cheese (about ¾ cup)
1	oz Parmesan cheese, shredded (about ¼ cup)
8	ozs fresh mozzarella, sliced
fresh basil	

1. In a 12" cast-iron skillet over medium heat, brown ground beef, sausage, and garlic. Remove meat mixture from skillet and set aside.

2. Add tomato sauce, diced tomatoes (including liquid), honey, Italian seasoning, pepper, basil, and rosemary to skillet. Bring to a simmer over medium heat.

3. Once sauce is simmering, add broken lasagna noodles. Reduce heat to medium-low and cook, stirring frequently, until lasagna noodles are tender (about 12 minutes). Add meat mixture back to the skillet, mix well, and remove pan from heat.

4. Preheat oven broiler.

5. In a small bowl, combine ricotta and Parmesan. Create divots in sauce and spoon in ricotta mixture. Cover ricotta with sauce, and arrange mozzarella slices on top of lasagna.

6. Broil lasagna just until mozzarella is melted and beginning to brown. If desired, serve with fresh, torn basil leaves.

15" x 12¼" Cast-Iron Rectangular Griddle

MEATLOAF PATTIES

These irresistible patties are combination of all the best parts of a meatloaf—crisp on the outside, tender on the inside, and each bite is smothered with a sweet and tangy glaze. Delish!

MAKES: 8 SERVINGS

Meatloaf Patties:

1½	lbs lean ground beef
½	onion, peeled and minced (about 1 cup)
2	garlic cloves, peeled and minced (about 2 t)
2	T fresh parsley, minced (about 1 T)
1	sprig rosemary, de-stemmed and minced (about ½ t)
¾	t salt
¼	t pepper
1	T Dijon mustard
¾	cup breadcrumbs
½	cup buttermilk
1	egg
¼	t baking soda (tenderizes the meat)
1	t water

Glaze:

½	cup ketchup
4	t brown sugar
2	t apple-cider vinegar
1	pinch cayenne pepper

1. In a large bowl, combine ground beef, onion, garlic, parsley, rosemary, salt, pepper, mustard, breadcrumbs, buttermilk, and egg; mix well. In a small bowl, combine baking soda and water. Add to meatloaf mixture and mix well.

2. Divide meatloaf mixture into 8 equal portions and shape into oval patties.

3. Preheat oven to 375°F.

4. In a large skillet over medium heat, fry patties in batches to for 3–5 minutes on each side, or until browned. Transfer patties to a 15" x 12¼" cast-iron griddle and set aside.

5. Make glaze: In a small bowl, combine ketchup, brown sugar, apple-cider vinegar, and cayenne. Evenly divide glaze between patties and spread over the tops.

6. Bake for 15 minutes, or until internal temperature reaches 160°F.

MaryJanesFarm

Farmgirls-in-Training

Petite Tomatoes

Organic Heirloom
ONE DRY PINT

MaryJanesFarm
Moscow, Idaho
MaryJanesFarm.org
208-882-6819

0 99853 28001 1

The future of organic agriculture depends on the next generation. For that matter, the future of my organic farm depends on my granddaughters, so I decided I'd get them acquainted with the business of selling organic produce at a very young age. Their excitement and enthusiasm and *skill* have been remarkable. When I bought my farm in 1986, I could only hope to end up with granddaughters as excited as I am about feeding people organic food. Thank you for sharing in our hopes and dreams and for your support of my granddaughters, Stella Jane, Adria Ruth, and Mia Marie.

MaryJane ♥

12" Cast-Iron Skillet

2   T butter, softened
2   T fresh cilantro, minced (1 T)
1   t lime zest
2   bell peppers, seeded, halved, and thinly sliced (about 2½ cups)
½   onion, peeled and thinly sliced (about 1 cup)
3   garlic cloves, peeled and minced (1 T)
1   t salt, divided
1   lb boneless, skinless chicken breast, thinly sliced
½   t paprika
½   t chili powder
¼   t pepper
⅛   t cayenne pepper
1   t coconut oil
12   6½" Tortillas, p. 80

CHICKEN FAJITAS

Fajitas, wrapped up in my homemade flour tortillas (p. 80), are the stuff daydreams are made of. When I think of these fajitas, I get lost anticipating the subtle coconut flavor of the tortillas pairing ever-so-perfectly with the cilantro and lime in the filling.

MAKES: 4 SERVINGS

1. In a small bowl, combine butter, cilantro, and lime zest; set aside.

2. In a medium bowl, combine bell peppers, onion, garlic, and ½ t salt.

3. In another medium bowl, combine chicken, remaining ½ t salt, paprika, chili powder, pepper, and cayenne pepper.

4. In a 12" cast-iron skillet over medium heat, melt coconut oil. Add chicken mixture and cook until heated through, stirring occasionally (about 10 minutes). Add pepper mixture and cook until tender-crisp (3–5 minutes); remove from heat.

5. Add butter mixture to skillet and mix in until melted. Serve on warm Tortillas, p. 80.

4-qt Cast-Iron Universal Pan

4 ozs bacon (about 4 slices), diced
1 lb boneless, skinless chicken breasts, finely diced
1¼ t salt, divided
¼ t pepper
1 leek, trimmed, halved, and sliced (about 1½ cups)
2¾ cups milk
¾ cup heavy cream
1 sprig rosemary
1½ lbs Yukon Gold potatoes
6 ozs shredded fontina cheese (about 1½ cups), divided
2 T cornstarch
2 T cold water

Special Equipment:

mandoline slicer

gluten free

POTATO, CHICKEN & BACON CASSEROLE

This casserole takes scalloped potatoes to the next level with the addition of chicken and bacon. In addition, the potatoes are cooked in rosemary-infused milk. Once the potatoes are tender, the milk is drained and used as the base for the sauce. Positively delicious!

MAKES: 8–10 SERVINGS

1. In a medium skillet over medium heat, cook bacon until crisp. Remove bacon from skillet and drain all but 2 t of bacon drippings from the pan. Add chicken, ¼ t salt, and pepper to skillet and cook over medium heat until chicken is cooked through. Remove from heat. Add chicken, bacon, and leek to a medium bowl; toss to combine and set aside.

2. In a medium saucepan over medium heat, bring milk, cream, rosemary, and remaining 1 t salt to a simmer.

3. While milk mixture is cooking, slice potatoes into ⅛"-thick slices using a mandoline slicer. Add potatoes to milk mixture and cook for 5–7 minutes, or until potatoes are tender-crisp.

4. Place a colander over a large bowl and drain milk mixture from potatoes. Remove rosemary sprig from potatoes and discard.

5. Preheat oven to 400°F. Butter a 4-qt cast-iron universal pan.

6. Add about ¼ of the chicken mixture to the bottom of the prepared pan. Top with a single layer of potatoes and ⅓ cup fontina cheese. Add another ¼ of the chicken mixture, another layer of potatoes, and ⅓ cup fontina cheese. Add another ¼ of the chicken mixture, another layer of potatoes, and ⅓ cup fontina cheese. For the final layer, use remaining chicken mixture, another single layer of potatoes, and remaining ½ cup fontina cheese.

7. Add strained milk mixture to a medium saucepan and bring to a simmer over medium-low heat. In a small bowl, mix cornstarch and cold water together. Pour into milk mixture and continue to cook over medium-low heat, stirring frequently, until thickened. Pour milk sauce over top of casserole. Bake for 20–25 minutes, until cheese is melted and bubbling.

10¼" Cast-Iron Skillet

Filling:

1	lb boneless, skinless chicken breasts
¾	t salt, divided
¼	t pepper
1	T safflower oil
4	garlic cloves, peeled and minced (about 4 t)
4	celery stalks, halved lengthwise and sliced (about 1 cup)
1	carrot, peeled, quartered, and sliced (about 1 cup)
2	cups chicken broth
2	T cornstarch
2	T cold water
½	cup fresh or thawed frozen peas
2	T sour cream

Biscuits:

1	half batch Buttermilk Biscuits, p. 88

Herb Butter:

1	T fresh parsley, minced
1	sprig rosemary, de-stemmed and minced (about ½ t)
¼	t fresh thyme, minced
1	T butter, melted

BISCUIT & CHICKEN SKILLET PIE

Chicken soup *and* biscuits, *crispy* biscuits, are truly the ultimate in comfort food. These biscuits, top dressed with fresh herbs and butter, take the comfort part of this meal to a whole new level.

MAKES: 8 SERVINGS

1. Sprinkle chicken breasts with ½ t salt and the pepper. In a 10¼" cast-iron skillet over medium heat, heat safflower oil. Add chicken and cook on one side for 5 minutes. Flip over and cook for an additional 5 minutes. Reduce heat to low, cover, and cook for 10 more minutes, or until internal temperature reaches 165°F. Transfer chicken to a cutting board to cool.

2. Add garlic, celery, and carrot to skillet used to cook chicken. Cook over medium heat until vegetables are tender-crisp. Add chicken broth and remaining ¼ t salt. Bring to a low simmer. In a small bowl, combine cornstarch and cold water. Pour into vegetable mixture and cook until mixture has thickened; remove from heat.

3. Dice chicken and add to pan. Mix in peas and sour cream; set pan aside.

4. Preheat oven to 425°F.

5. Prep a half batch of Buttermilk Biscuit dough, p. 88. On a lightly floured surface, roll dough into a 10" circle and cut eight 3" biscuits (you'll have some scraps left over).

6. Arrange biscuits on top of chicken filling. Bake for 15 minutes, or until biscuits are golden brown.

7. In the meantime, make herb butter: In a small bowl, combine parsley, rosemary, thyme, and butter. Brush over tops of biscuits and serve immediately.

PASTOR'S PIE

MAKES: 8 SERVINGS

5-qt Cast-Iron Dutch Oven

Filling:

4–5	lb whole chicken
5	garlic cloves
1½	onions, peeled, divided
1	bunch celery, sliced (about 4 cups), reserve bottom
2	t salt, divided
1½	t pepper, divided
2	T safflower oil
2	carrots, sliced (about 2 cups)
2	T cornstarch
2	T cold water
2	cups peas fresh or thawed frozen

Biscuits:

1	half batch Buttermilk Biscuits, p. 88

1. Preheat oven to 450°F. Remove the giblet package from the inside of the chicken and discard.

2. Stuff the cavity of the chicken with 5 whole, unpeeled garlic cloves, half an onion, and the bottom portion of the celery bunch.

3. Rub the outside of the chicken with 1 t salt and ¾ t pepper. In a 5-qt lidded Dutch oven, heat safflower oil over medium-high heat for 2 minutes.

4. Place the whole chicken into the Dutch oven, uncovered, and sear both sides for 5 minutes each.

5. Remove the Dutch oven from heat, cover, and bake, breast side down, at 450°F for 1 hour, or until internal temperature of the legs reaches 165°F.

6. Once the chicken is cooked, remove from oven, remove the lid, and allow it to cool.

7. When the chicken has cooled enough to handle, remove it from the Dutch oven, leaving the pan drippings inside the Dutch oven.

8. Remove all of the meat from the chicken and cut it into small pieces. Preheat oven to 450°F.

9. Over medium heat, reheat the pan drippings inside the Dutch oven.

10. Dice the remaining onion and add it to the pan; cook for 3 minutes. Then add sliced celery. Allow mixture to cook for 5 minutes, then stir in the sliced carrots and cook for an additional 5 minutes.

11. In a small bowl, combine cornstarch and water. Slowly pour the cornstarch into the Dutch oven and cook until mixture has thickened; remove from heat.

12. Add the diced chicken, peas, remaining 1 t salt, and remaining ¾ t pepper to the Dutch oven. Stir to combine.

13. Prepare a half batch of Buttermilk Biscuit dough, p. 88.

14. On a lightly floured surface, roll out biscuit dough to ¼" thickness. Use the Dutch oven lid to stamp a depression in the dough to make a topping that fits perfectly over the top of the pie.

15. Bake at 450°F, uncovered, for 20 minutes, or until biscuit topping is golden brown.

Ever heard of Pastor's Pie? Aiming to please, the women of a congregation would deliver to their pastor one of their prize-winning best. His favorite, as it turns out, involved a chicken and a Dutch oven. The instructions for this recipe might seem fussy, but trust me, it's well worth the effort.

8" Cast-Iron Skillet

3   garlic cloves, peeled and minced (about 1 T)
1½ cups milk
½   cup dry polenta
1   T fresh dill, minced (about 1½ t), plus more for garnish
½   t salt, divided
½   onion, peeled and thinly sliced (about 1 cup)
2   t olive oil
8   ozs Brussels sprouts, halved and thinly sliced (about 2¾ cups)
6   ozs crimini mushrooms, halved and thinly sliced (about 1½ cups)
4   ozs Havarti cheese, shredded (about ½ cup)

gluten free

Baked Polenta with Brussels Sprouts and Mushrooms

Sometimes, when I mull over my dinner options, I'm caught up in the idea of something warm and comforting. It was on one of those nights that I cooked up this dish, and it's since turned into a regular dinner staple.

MAKES: 4 SERVINGS

1. Preheat oven to 400°F.

2. In an 8" cast-iron skillet over medium heat, toast garlic until fragrant. Add milk and bring to a boil. Mix in polenta, dill, and ¼ t salt; reduce heat to low. Cook until polenta has thickened; remove from heat, and set aside.

3. In a medium skillet over medium heat, sauté onion in olive oil until soft. Add Brussels sprouts, mushrooms, and remaining ¼ t salt. Cook until mushrooms are soft, stirring frequently.

4. Transfer sautéed vegetables to pan with polenta, and spread out evenly. Top with Havarti and bake for 8–10 minutes, or until cheese is bubbling and beginning to brown. If using, garnish with minced fresh dill and serve.

8" Cast-Iron Skillet

ASPARAGUS & MUSHROOM QUICHE WITH POTATO CRUST

I seriously wanted to call this the best thing that had ever come out of my kitchen when I first tasted it. The potato crust, crispy to the max, ensures you'll come back to this recipe time and time again. Let's not ask how many times I've pulled this one from my bag of tricks.

MAKES: ONE 8" QUICHE

Russet Crust:

1	large russet potato (about 1 lb)
1	T olive oil
½	t salt
¼	t pepper
¾	oz Parmesan cheese, grated (about 3 T)
¼	t dried rosemary

Filling:

4	ozs bacon (about 4 slices)
6	ozs crimini mushrooms, halved and sliced (about 1½ cups)
1	clove garlic, peeled and minced (about 1 t)
20	asparagus spears, cut into 1" pieces (about 2 cups)
2	ozs Havarti cheese, shredded (about ½ cup), divided
2	ozs Cheddar cheese, shredded (about ½ cup), divided
6	eggs
2	T milk

Special Equipment:

mandoline slicer

1. Preheat oven to 450°F.

2. Peel and slice potato using mandoline slicer to ⅛" thickness; add to a medium bowl. Add remaining crust ingredients and mix well.

3. Arrange potato slices around the bottom and sides of an 8" cast-iron skillet. Bake for 20 minutes.

4. While the crust is baking, dice bacon and add to a medium skillet. Cook over medium heat until crisp (about 7 minutes), remove bacon, and drain all but 1 T of the grease. Add mushrooms and garlic and cook until tender. Remove from heat and mix in asparagus and bacon.

5. Remove crust from oven and reduce oven temperature to 350°F.

6. Add about half of the mushroom mixture to bottom of crust, then add about half of the Havarti and Cheddar. Add remaining mushroom mixture and top with remaining Havarti and Cheddar.

7. In a medium bowl, whisk eggs and milk together; pour over cheeses.

8. Place quiche on a large baking sheet, bake for 35–40 minutes, or until eggs have set.

gluten
free

9-oz Cast Iron Oval Mini-Server
(Note: this recipe calls for 6 mini-servers)

Marinated Broccoli Sprouts:

1	T red wine vinegar
2	t olive oil
1	t honey
⅛	t salt
4	ozs broccoli sprouts (about 3 cups)

Beef, Zucchini & Polenta Casserole:

1	lb ground beef
2	zucchini, quartered and sliced ⅛" thick (about 3½ cups)
½	fennel bulb, trimmed and diced (about 1 cup)
1	14.5-oz can diced tomatoes, drained
2½	t salt, divided
½	t pepper
3	cups water
¾	cup dry polenta
3	ozs crumbled feta (about ⅓ cup)
2	T fresh oregano leaves, minced
2	sprigs fresh rosemary, de-stemmed and minced (about 1 t)

gluten free

BEEF, ZUCCHINI & POLENTA MINI CASSEROLES WITH MARINATED BROCCOLI SPROUTS

I love the versatility of polenta. It adapts to dishes both sweet and savory with ease, and it pairs well with just about anything. These mini casseroles definitely deliver flavor, and since they're quick to prepare, are a great choice for a weeknight meal.

MAKES: 6 SERVINGS

1. Preheat oven to 350°F. Arrange six 9-oz cast-iron oval mini-servers on a large baking sheet.

2. Make marinated broccoli sprouts: In a medium bowl, whisk vinegar, olive oil, honey, and salt together. Add broccoli sprouts and toss to coat. Cover and refrigerate.

3. Make casserole: In a large skillet, brown ground beef over medium heat; drain. Add zucchini, fennel, tomatoes, 1½ t salt, and pepper. Continue to cook over medium heat until fennel is softened and zucchini is tender-crisp; remove from heat and divide mixture evenly between mini-servers.

4. In a medium saucepan, bring water and remaining 1 t salt to a boil. Whisk in polenta; cook until thickened, stirring frequently. Remove from heat and stir in feta, oregano, and rosemary.

5. Evenly divide polenta mixture between oval mini-servers and bake for 15 minutes. Serve with marinated broccoli sprouts.

12" Cast-Iron Skillet

1½   lbs bone-in chicken thighs
1½   lbs chicken legs
1   t salt
½   t pepper
½   t fresh thyme leaves
1   T safflower oil
1   lb yellow potatoes, cut into 1"
     cubes (about 2¾ cups)
1   red onion, peeled, halved, and
     sliced into ½"-thick pieces
     (about 2 cups)
½   cup chicken broth
½   cup buttermilk
¼   cup fresh tarragon

gluten free

Skillet-Roasted Chicken with Potatoes & Tarragon

If there's ever been a dish that I'd call picture-perfect, it's this one. I clearly remember pulling this entrée from my oven, sprinkling it with tarragon, placing it on the table, and being somewhat awestruck by its simple beauty.

MAKES: 4–6 SERVINGS

1. Preheat oven to 400°F.

2. In a large bowl, combine chicken with salt, pepper, and thyme.

3. Add oil to a 12" cast-iron skillet and heat over medium-high heat.

4. Once oil is hot, add chicken, skin-side down, alternating between thighs and drumsticks. Sear for 8–10 minutes, until skin is golden. Flip chicken pieces over and remove from heat.

5. Add potatoes and onion slices, tucking some pieces under the chicken. Pour chicken broth and buttermilk over all ingredients in skillet.

6. Bake for about 40 minutes, or until potatoes are tender and chicken reaches an internal temperature of 165°F. Just before serving, sprinkle with fresh tarragon leaves.

FRIED CHICKEN

What's better than fried chicken? Fried chicken that's been marinated in buttermilk, dill, and garlic, then dredged in flour and fried in a cast-iron skillet, of course! Even better, the addition of baking powder and baking soda give the breading a little lift as the chicken cooks, creating a light, crisp crust.

MAKES: 6 SERVINGS

Marinade:

2	cups buttermilk
¼	cup dill, minced
4	garlic cloves, peeled and minced (about 4 t)
2	t salt
2½	lbs bone-in chicken pieces (any assortment of breasts, wings, thighs, and legs)

Breading:

¾	cup flour
¼	cup corn flour
1½	t paprika
½	t baking powder
½	t baking soda
½	t salt
½	t celery seed
¼	t pepper
⅔	cup safflower oil

1. Prepare marinade: In a medium bowl, combine buttermilk, dill, garlic, and salt. Add chicken pieces, cover, and refrigerate for at least 4 hours.

2. Place a cooling rack over a large baking sheet and set aside.

3. Prepare breading: In a shallow bowl or pie plate, combine flour, corn flour, paprika, baking powder, baking soda, salt, celery seed, and pepper. Remove chicken pieces from marinade, shaking off excess buttermilk. Dredge each piece in flour mixture and place on prepared cooling rack.

4. Preheat oven to 400°F.

5. In a 12" cast-iron skillet over medium heat, heat safflower oil. Once oil is hot, add chicken pieces in batches and fry on both sides until chicken is evenly browned. After browning, transfer chicken pieces to a 15" x 12¼" cast-iron rectangular griddle. Bake for 20–25 minutes, or until internal temperature reaches 165°F, covering with foil halfway through to prevent over-browning.

10¼" Cast-Iron Skillet

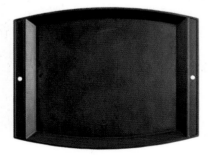

15" x 12¼" Cast-Iron Rectangular Griddle

1	lb boneless, skinless chicken breasts
2	t fresh lime juice (about ½ lime)
1	t salt, divided
¼	t pepper
¼	t chili powder
1	t safflower oil
1	cup cooked brown rice
1	15-oz can black beans, rinsed and drained (about 1¾ cups)
¾	cup fresh or thawed frozen corn
⅓	cup fresh cilantro leaves, minced
½	jalapeño pepper, seeded and diced (about 1 T)
4	garlic cloves, peeled and minced (about 4 t)
8	ozs Monterey jack cheese, shredded (about 2 cups), divided
½	cup sour cream
¼	cup chicken broth
1	tomato, diced (about ⅔ cup)
4	green onions, sliced (about 6 T)

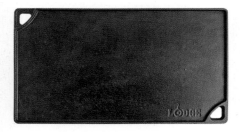

Cast-Iron Grill/Griddle

10¼" Cast-Iron Skillet

CREAMY GRILLED CHICKEN & RICE CASSEROLE

I strongly contend that nothing cooks chicken better than cast iron. I especially love the way my cast-iron grill pan leaves golden-brown grill marks on the chicken as it cooks.

MAKES: 6 SERVINGS

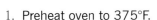

1. Preheat oven to 375°F.

2. In a medium bowl, toss chicken breasts with lime juice, ½ t salt, pepper, and chili powder.

3. Add oil to a cast-iron grill and heat over medium heat. Once oil is hot, add chicken and cook on each side for 6–8 minutes, until chicken reaches an internal temperature of 165°F; remove from heat.

4. Cool chicken slightly, cut into ½" cubes, and transfer to a medium bowl. Add rice, beans, corn, cilantro, jalapeño, garlic, and 1 cup Monterey jack cheese; mix well.

5. In a small bowl, whisk sour cream, chicken broth, and remaining ½ t salt together. Stir into chicken mixture.

6. Transfer mixture to a 10¼" cast-iron skillet, top with remaining cheese, and bake for 50–55 minutes, until heated through and cheese is melted and bubbly. Serve with diced tomato and green onions.

10¼" Cast-Iron Skillet

Crust:

2¼	cups white rice flour
¾	cup tapioca flour
2	t baking powder
1	t baking soda
1	t salt
1½	cups milk
2	eggs
¼	cup coconut oil, melted

Toppings:

2	large yellow bell peppers, seeded and cut into ¼"-thick rings
2	yellow summer squash, cut diagonally into ¼" slices (about 3 cups sliced)
3	garlic cloves, peeled and minced (about 1 T)
2	t olive oil
1	t Italian seasoning
½	t salt
4	ozs sliced salami
2	ozs Parmesan cheese, shredded (about ½ cup)
3	ozs feta cheese, crumbled (about ⅓ cup)

fresh basil for garnish

Tomato & Cashew Sauce:

¾	cup fresh basil leaves
½	cup oil-packed sun-dried tomatoes
¼	cup cashews
1	oz Parmesan cheese (about ¼ cup)
¼	cup olive oil
½	t salt

Pizza Crust with Roasted Peppers & Summer Squash

A nice, summery twist on pizza that's packed with flavor. The Tomato & Cashew Sauce lends excellent flavor to the pizza, and the abundant toppings are sure to satisfy.

MAKES: 6 SERVINGS

1. Preheat oven to 425°F. Generously butter a 10¼" cast-iron skillet.

2. Make crust: In a medium bowl, combine rice flour, tapioca flour, baking powder, baking soda, and salt. Make a well in the center and add milk, eggs, and coconut oil. Stir until dough forms.

3. Spoon dough into prepared skillet and press into the bottom and up the sides (to make forming easier, periodically wet fingers); set aside.

4. Prepare vegetable toppings: Add peppers, squash, garlic, olive oil, Italian seasoning, and salt to a medium bowl. Mix well and transfer to a 9" x 13" baking dish. Bake uncovered for 15 minutes.

5. While vegetables are baking, prepare sauce: Add all ingredients to a food processor and pulse until puréed. Spread over the bottom and up the sides of crust.

6. Layer about half of the peppers and squash mixture over crust, then add salami. Layer remaining peppers and squash mixture; top with Parmesan and feta. Bake for 25 minutes, or until crust is golden brown. Garnish with torn basil leaves.

12" Cast-Iron Skillet

Crust:

¾	cup warm water
2	T olive oil
1	t honey
1	package active dry yeast (about 2¼ t)
1¾	cups flour, plus more for dusting
¼	cup semolina flour
½	t salt

Toppings:

½	cup pizza sauce
8	ozs mozzarella cheese, shredded (about 2 cups), divided
3	ozs sliced pepperoni
½	green bell pepper, seeded and diced (about ⅔ cup)
¼	cup sliced black olives

DEEP-DISH PIZZA

The crust for this pizza has just the right combination of crunch and chew. Topped with classic pizza toppings and just the right amount of cheese, what isn't there to love?

MAKES: ONE 12" PIZZA

1. Make crust: In a small bowl, combine warm water, olive oil, and honey; whisk until honey is dissolved (mixture shouldn't feel hot on the inside of your wrist). Whisk in yeast and set aside.

2. Add flour, semolina flour, and salt to a stand mixer fitted with a dough hook. Make a depression in the center of the flour to receive the liquid; add yeast mixture to flour.

3. Mix until dough forms, and continue to mix until dough is smooth and pliable (5–8 minutes).

4. Lightly oil a medium bowl with olive oil. Dust hands and dough with flour and shape dough into a ball. Place in prepared bowl, cover with plastic wrap, and let rise in a warm place for 1½ hours, or until doubled in bulk.

5. Preheat oven to 425°F. Generously butter a 12" cast-iron skillet.

6. Deflate dough. On a lightly floured surface, roll dough out into a 15" circle. Transfer dough to prepared skillet and roll up edges to form a crust. With the tip of a fork, poke a few holes in the bottom of the crust (this helps prevent air pockets from forming under the crust).

7. Pre-bake crust for 10 minutes. Remove from oven and cool slightly.

8. Add toppings: Spread pizza sauce over bottom of crust. Add about ½ cup of cheese, all the pepperoni, and another ½ cup of cheese. Add peppers and olives; top with remaining 1 cup cheese.

9. Bake for 15–18 minutes, until crust is a deep golden brown and cheese is bubbling and lightly browned in spots. Cool slightly and serve.

Filling:

3	ozs bacon (about 3 slices), diced
3	green onions, thinly sliced (about ½ cup)
1	lb boneless, skinless chicken breasts, diced
¼	t celery seed

salt and pepper to taste

1	cup green beans, sliced into ½" pieces
6	ozs button mushrooms, halved and sliced (about 1½ cups)
2	T flour
1	cup chicken broth
¼	cup heavy cream
2	ozs kale, coarsely diced (about 2 cups)

Crust:

1¼	cups flour
½	t salt
1	t baking powder
2	T butter
½	cup buttermilk

12" Cast-Iron Skillet

Enameled Cast-Iron Mini
Oval Cocotte
(Note: this recipe calls for 4 cocottes)

CREAMY CHICKEN SINGLE-SERVE POT PIE

I enjoy using my enameled cocottes to make single-serve meals. With classic flavors and a cute presentation, this pot pie is an all-around winner.

MAKES: 4 POT PIES

1. In a 12" cast-iron skillet over medium heat, cook bacon and green onions until bacon is nearly cooked. Add chicken, celery seed, and salt and pepper to skillet. Continue to cook until chicken is cooked through. Add green beans and mushrooms and cook for 3–5 minutes. Sprinkle in flour and cook for 1–2 minutes. Pour in chicken broth and cook until thickened (about 5 minutes). Remove from heat and stir in cream and kale. Divide filling evenly between four enameled cast-iron mini oval cocottes.

2. Preheat oven to 425°F. Combine flour, salt, and baking powder in a medium bowl. Cut in butter until mixture resembles coarse meal. Mix in buttermilk.

3. Roll out dough. Using a mini oval cocotte lid as a template, cut out 4 ovals for tops. Place dough over filling and cut slits in the top of each crust to allow steam to escape.

4. Place cocottes on a large baking sheet and bake for 18–20 minutes or until crusts are golden brown.

CHORIZO & RED BEAN SINGLE-SERVE POT PIE

This pot pie has a secret. You see the top? That's actually two layers of crust filled with Monterey jack cheese, begging to be dipped into the spicy chorizo and red bean filling.

MAKES: 6 POT PIES

1. Brown chorizo in a 10¼" cast-iron skillet over medium heat; drain.

2. In a medium saucepan, combine oil, carrot, celery, green pepper, onion, zucchini, and garlic; cook over medium heat until tender-crisp (3–5 minutes). Stir in chorizo, beans, chili powder, and salt and pepper. Evenly divide filling between six enameled cast-iron mini oval cocottes.

3. Preheat oven to 425°F. Make crust: In a medium bowl, combine flour, corn flour, salt, and baking powder. Cut in butter until mixture resembles coarse meal. Mix in buttermilk and honey.

4. Roll out dough. Using a mini oval cocotte lid as a template, cut out 12 ovals for tops. Evenly divide cheese between 6 ovals, top with remaining 6 ovals. Place dough over filling and cut slits in the top of each crust to allow steam to escape.

5. Place cocottes on a large baking sheet, brush with milk, and bake for 20–25 minutes or until crusts are golden brown.

Filling:

1	lb ground chorizo
1	T olive oil
1	carrot, thinly sliced (about 1 cup)
1	celery stalk, thinly sliced (about ¼ cup)
1	green bell pepper, seeded and diced (about 1¼ cup)
½	yellow onion, peeled and diced (about 1 cup)
1	zucchini, quartered and sliced (about 1½ cups)
2	cloves garlic, peeled and minced (about 2 t)
1	15 oz can red beans, drained and rinsed (1¾ cups)
½	t chili powder

salt and pepper to taste

Crust:

1	cup flour
¼	cup corn flour
½	t salt
1	t baking powder
2	T butter
½	cup buttermilk
1	T honey
3	ozs Monterey Jack cheese, shredded (about ¾ cup)
2	T milk

10¼" Cast-Iron Skillet

Enameled Cast-Iron Mini Oval Cocotte
(Note: this recipe calls for 6 cocottes)

2 T coconut oil
1½ lbs boneless, skinless chicken breasts, diced
5 garlic cloves, peeled and minced (about 5 t)
1 jalapeño, seeded and minced (about 2 T)
1 t salt, divided
⅛ t pepper
¼ t cayenne pepper
8 ozs button mushrooms, quartered (about 2 cups)
1⅔ cups sour cream
12 ozs Monterey jack, shredded (about 3 cups)
fresh cilantro for garnish
Tortillas, p. 80
cooked brown rice
grilled bell peppers

12" Cast-Iron Skillet

Optional: Enameled Cast-Iron Mini Round Cocotte
(Note: this recipe calls for 6 cocottes)

CHICKEN & CREAM MEXICANA

One of my all-time faves, this dish is pure joy to eat. From the creamy sauce, to the wonderful texture of the chicken and mushrooms, rounded out with just the right amount of heat, I will always sing nothing but high praises for this dish.

MAKES: 6 SERVINGS

1. In a 12" cast-iron skillet over medium heat, combine oil, chicken, garlic, jalapeño, ½ t salt, pepper, and cayenne pepper. When chicken is mostly cooked, add mushrooms and cook until mushrooms are tender; remove from heat.

2. While the chicken and mushrooms are cooking, heat sour cream and remaining ½ t salt in a large saucepan over medium-low heat; stirring constantly.

3. Once sour cream is hot, slowly begin adding cheese, stirring well after each addition. Stir in chicken and mushroom mixture, including resulting liquid.

4. Serve with Tortillas (p. 80), brown rice, and grilled bell peppers.

Optional: For a pretty presentation, evenly divide mixture between six enameled cast-iron mini round cocottes and place on a large baking sheet. Bake at 375°F for 10–15 minutes, or until sauce is bubbling and tops begin to brown.

150

10¼" Cast-Iron Skillet

1   lb boneless, skinless
      chicken breasts
1   cup unsweetened, full-fat
      coconut milk, divided
2   T creamy peanut butter
2   T fresh lemon juice
      (about 1 lemon)
1   garlic clove, peeled and minced
      (about 1 t)
1   t curry powder
¼   t red pepper flakes
½   t salt, divided
1   T butter
1   cup couscous
1½   cups low-sodium chicken broth
chard
fresh cilantro for serving

gluten free

Coconut Curry Chicken Couscous

Easy to make and full of flavor, my recipe for Coconut Curry Chicken Couscous was a fast favorite here at the farm. Pair it with steamed chard, mix it all up, and dinner is on.

MAKES: 6 SERVINGS

1. Cut chicken crosswise into ¼"-thick strips; set aside.

2. In a medium bowl, combine ½ cup coconut milk, peanut butter, lemon juice, garlic, curry, red pepper flakes, and ¼ t salt. Stir mixture until smooth and creamy. Add chicken and mix well.

3. In a 10¼" cast-iron skillet, melt butter over medium-high heat and add chicken mixture. Cook, stirring occasionally, for 8–10 minutes, or until chicken is cooked through.

4. While chicken is cooking, in a medium saucepan over medium heat, combine couscous, chicken broth, remaining ½ cup coconut milk, and remaining ½ t salt. Bring to a boil and cook for 2 minutes. Remove from heat, cover, and let sit for 5 minutes, or until all liquid has been absorbed. Serve immediately with chicken. Garnish with cilantro. This dish is delicious paired with steamed chard or a garden salad.

153

12" Cast-Iron Skillet

2   8-oz tenderloin steaks
salt and pepper
1   T safflower oil
8   oz crimini or button mushrooms, sliced (about 2 cups)
1   shallot, peeled and minced (about ¼ cup)
½   cup pomegranate juice
½   cup low-sodium chicken broth
1   t Dijon mustard
¼   cup heavy cream
3   T cold butter
1½   T fresh thyme, minced (about 1 T)
salt and pepper to taste

gluten free

Pan-Seared Steaks with Pomegranate Mushroom Sauce

Whenever I am craving a steak, I always turn to my trusty cast-iron skillet. I can't imagine frying up a steak in any other pan. For this recipe, after the steaks are fried, I use the pan and drippings to make a delectable Pomegranate Mushroom Sauce to smother my steak.

MAKES: 2 SERVINGS

1. Pat steaks dry with a paper towel and season both sides of steaks generously with salt and pepper. Allow to sit at room temperature for 15–30 minutes.

2. Heat a 12" cast-iron skillet over high heat until hot and add the oil. Reduce heat to medium high, place steaks in pan and sear for 4 minutes without moving. Flip steaks and sear on other side until internal temperature reads 120–125°F for rare, 130–135°F for medium-rare, 140–145°F for medium-well, and 155–160°F for well-done.

3. Transfer to a plate and tent with foil to keep warm while preparing sauce.

4. Add sliced mushrooms to pan, and sauté over medium heat until brown and softened, about 5 minutes. Add shallot and cook for 1 minute. Increase heat to high and add pomegranate juice and chicken broth to the pan, scraping up the brown bits with a wooden spoon. Simmer rapidly until liquid is reduced by half, about 6–8 minutes.

5. Add mustard, cream, and any accumulated steak juices from plate and simmer until sauce coats the back of a spoon, about 2–3 minutes.

6. Remove from heat, stir in butter and thyme, and season with salt and pepper to taste. Spoon sauce over steaks and serve immediately.

GARLIC SMASHED POTATOES

MAKES: 2 SERVINGS

1. Place potatoes in a medium saucepan and cover with water. Bring to a boil over high heat; reduce heat and simmer until potatoes are tender, about 20 minutes.

2. While potatoes are cooking, place whole garlic cloves in a dry 10¼" cast-iron skillet over low heat, tossing frequently until soft, about 20 minutes. Peel and mash into a paste with the back of a spoon.

3. Drain potatoes and add to skillet along with garlic paste. Using a potato masher, mash potatoes until smooth. Add butter and half-and-half; mix until thoroughly combined. Stir in chives, and season with salt and pepper to taste.

10¼" Cast-Iron Skillet

1½	lbs potatoes, peeled and cut into 2" cubes (about 4 cups)
10	cloves garlic, skins left on
4	T butter, softened
½	cup half-and-half, warm
2	T minced fresh chives
salt and pepper to taste	

gluten free

HAM DINNER ON THE HALF PEEL

A twist on traditional twice-baked potatoes, this recipe, featuring sweet potatoes, makes a great entrée served with a big salad. It also makes a great accompaniment to grilled chicken or steak.

MAKES: 4 SERVINGS

2	sweet potatoes (about 2 lbs)
20	pecan halves
1	T maple syrup
¼	cup sour cream
2	T butter
6	ozs cooked ham, cut into ¼" cubes (about 1 cup)
½	cup fresh or frozen peas

10¼" Cast-Iron Skillet

9" x 13" Cast-Iron Baking Pan

gluten free

1. Preheat oven to 350°F.

2. Wash potatoes and cut off ends; do not dry. Place potatoes in a 10¼" cast-iron skillet and bake for 1 hour, 15 minutes, or until potatoes are tender.

3. While potatoes are cooking, heat a small skillet over medium heat. Add pecans and maple syrup. Cook pecans, stirring constantly until syrup becomes candied (about 5 minutes). Remove from heat and set aside.

4. Once potatoes are tender, remove from oven. Set aside until cool enough to handle (about 15 minutes).

5. When potatoes are cool, cut each potato in half lengthwise. Run a sharp knife about ¼" in from the outside edge along each potato half (this will keep a little flesh in the potato, which helps them hold their shape). Scoop out potato flesh and place in a medium bowl; set skins aside. Add sour cream and butter to potato flesh; mix until smooth and creamy. Add ham and peas and mix well.

6. Place potato skins into a 9" x 13" cast-iron baking pan and fill with potato mixture. Arrange candied pecan halves on top. Bake for an additional 15 minutes.

5-qt Cast-Iron Dutch Oven

1	lb elbow macaroni
7	T butter, divided
1	yellow onion, peeled and thinly sliced
¼	cup flour
3	cups milk
16	ozs Colby-jack cheese, shredded (about 4 cups)
8	ozs sharp Cheddar cheese, shredded (about 2 cups)
¼	t salt

Mac & Cheese

With flavorful, caramelized onions; velvety, cheesy sauce; and not too many or too few macaroni noodles, this dish drives the point home on exactly what made mac & cheese such a classic, beloved staple.

MAKES: 8 SERVINGS

1. Preheat oven to 375°F.

2. Bring a large saucepan of water to a boil; add macaroni, and cook for 7–9 minutes, or until al dente. Drain and set aside.

3. While macaroni is cooking, melt 3 T butter in a 5-qt cast-iron Dutch oven over medium heat. Add onion slices and cook for 15 minutes, stirring occasionally. Remove onions from Dutch oven and set aside.

4. Melt remaining 4 T butter in Dutch oven over medium heat. Add flour and stir until a paste forms.

5. Continuing to cook over medium heat, gradually add milk, stirring constantly. Once all milk has been added and sauce has thickened, add cheeses and salt and continue to cook until completely melted.

6. Mix macaroni into sauce and top with onions.

7. Cover and bake for 45 minutes.

12" Cast-Iron Skillet

Stir Fry:

1	lb boneless bottom round roast
1	T brown sugar
3	garlic cloves, peeled and minced (about 1 T)
1	t fresh grated ginger
¾	t salt
¼	t crushed red pepper
1	T safflower oil
10	ozs fresh broccoli florets (about 4 cups)
1	red bell pepper, seeded and cut into ¼" x 2" strips (about 1¼ cups)

cooked brown rice for serving (optional)

Stir-fry Sauce:

2	T soy sauce
1	T brown sugar
1	T mirin
1	t toasted sesame oil
1½	t cornstarch

BEEF & BROCCOLI STIR FRY

The key to this dish is slicing the beef as thinly as possible. A little tip? Pop the roast in the freezer for about 1 hour before slicing. This will firm up the meat so it doesn't buckle under the pressure of your knife. Each time I make this entrée, I enjoy the vibrant, contrasting colors of the red bell peppers and the broccoli florets.

MAKES: 4–6 SERVINGS

1. Slice roast into ⅛"–¼"-thick slices and add to a medium bowl. Add brown sugar, garlic, ginger, salt, and crushed red pepper to bowl with beef; toss to combine. Cover bowl and refrigerate for 2 hours.

2. After 2 hours, prepare stir-fry sauce: In a small bowl, combine soy sauce, brown sugar, mirin, toasted sesame oil, and cornstarch. Mix well and set aside.

3. Add safflower oil to a 12" cast-iron skillet and heat over medium-low heat until oil is shimmering. Add beef mixture and cook, stirring occasionally until meat is cooked (about 8–10 minutes).

4. Add broccoli, bell pepper, and stir-fry sauce to pan and continue to cook over medium-low heat until broccoli is tender (about 3–4 minutes). Enjoy immediately as a stand-alone dish, or if desired, serve over cooked brown rice.

gluten free

10¼" Cast-Iron Skillet

1½	lbs chicken legs
¾	t salt, divided
¼	t pepper
¼	t crushed red pepper
2	t toasted sesame oil
¾	cup orange juice
1	T cornstarch
1	T honey
1	T distilled white vinegar
1	red bell pepper, seeded and sliced into ¼"-thick strips (about 1¼ cups)
1	t sesame seeds
2	green onions, sliced (about ⅓ cup)

gluten free

SESAME ORANGE CHICKEN LEGS

In addition to being pleasing to the eye, this dish is a sure palate-pleaser. As the chicken bakes, the juices cook into the orange sauce, creating plenty of wonderfully flavored sauce to slather all over the chicken legs.

MAKES: 4–6 SERVINGS

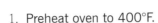

1. Preheat oven to 400°F.

2. Place chicken on a plate. In a small bowl, combine ¼ t salt, pepper, and crushed red pepper. Sprinkle about half of seasoning mixture over chicken legs, flip legs over, and sprinkle with remaining seasoning mixture.

3. In a 10¼" cast-iron skillet over medium heat, heat sesame oil. When oil is hot, add chicken legs. Cook without moving for 6 minutes, flip over, and cook an additional 6 minutes. Transfer skillet to preheated oven and cook for 10 minutes.

4. While chicken is cooking, combine orange juice and cornstarch in a small saucepan; whisk to combine. Add honey and remaining ½ t salt. Bring to a simmer over medium heat, whisking frequently. Once sauce has thickened, remove from heat and whisk in vinegar.

5. Remove chicken from oven and add sliced peppers. Pour orange sauce over chicken and bake for 25–30 minutes, or until internal temperature of chicken reaches 165°F.

6. In a dry skillet over medium heat, toast sesame seeds until golden brown. Remove from heat and cool slightly.

7. Sprinkle sesame seeds and green onions over chicken and serve.

14" Cast-Iron Wok

4   T butter, divided
4   garlic cloves, peeled and
    minced (about 4 t)
¾   lb boneless pork chops,
    finely diced
1   t salt
2   eggs, lightly beaten
3   cups cooked, cold jasmine rice
    (rice will retain its shape best
    if it has been refrigerated
    overnight)
⅔   cup frozen peas
2   T miso
⅓   cup fresh cilantro leaves,
    minced (about 3 T)
1   T lime juice (about 1
    small lime)
½   t toasted sesame oil
3   green onions, sliced
    (about ½ cup)

PORK FRIED RICE

For best results, cook the rice for this recipe at least a day ahead of time and refrigerate it. This step will help the rice retain its shape. The addition of miso is critical to the flavor of this dish. It adds the perfect umami touch to the fried rice.

MAKES: 4–6 SERVINGS

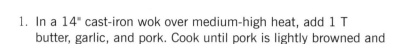

1. In a 14" cast-iron wok over medium-high heat, add 1 T butter, garlic, and pork. Cook until pork is lightly browned and cooked through; add salt and transfer to a bowl.

2. Continuing to cook over medium-high heat, add eggs to pan and cook until set. Add eggs to bowl with pork.

3. Continuing over medium-high heat, add remaining 3 T butter, rice, peas, and miso. Cook for about 3 minutes, stirring frequently. Remove from heat and add pork and egg mixture, cilantro, lime juice, and sesame oil; mix well. Serve with green onions.

The traditional Chinese wok, often made of hammered steel with a rounded bottom, lent its genius to this early cast-iron beauty. The bottom allows you to easily toss things quickly over a hot burner or fire, but its deep design also allows room for steaming, poaching, and stewing, plus the vintage version of a wok has a side handle. Did I mention, versatility is Miss Wok's middle name?

SECTION 5
SWEETS & DESSERTS

Cast-Iron Mini-Cake Pan

MINI APPLE PIES

The next time you're asked to provide tasties for a bake sale, this is your go-to recipe. Everything about these little mini pies speaks not only clever and playful, but Crust with a capital C. You'll never go back to a normal pie once you eat a serving of apple pie designed to give you a generous helping of crispy crust with every bite, like only cast iron can deliver.

MAKES: 7 MINI PIES

Crust:

Large Butter Cookie Pie Crust, p. 186

Apple Filling:

1½	lbs Granny Smith apples, peeled, cored, thinly sliced, and cut into 1/2"-wide pieces (about 3 cups)
½	cup sugar, plus more for sprinkling tops of pies
⅓	cup flour, plus more for dusting
½	t cinnamon
¼	t nutmeg
¼	t ground ginger
⅓	cup apple juice

1. Make Large Butter Cookie Pie Crust, as directed on p. 186.

2. Make apple filling: Add apples to a medium bowl; set aside. In a small bowl, combine sugar, flour, cinnamon, nutmeg, and ginger. Add sugar mixture to apples; mix well.

3. In a small saucepan, bring apple juice to a boil. Pour into apple mixture; mix well. Let stand while rolling out pie crust.

4. Preheat oven to 400°F. Lightly butter cups of cast-iron mini-cake pan and place on a large baking sheet.

5. On a floured surface roll out one disc of pie crust to ⅛" thickness. Cut pie crust into seven 5" circles. Place one circle in each pan cup and press into the bottom and up the sides.

6. Evenly divide apple filling between pan cavities, reserving about 1 T liquid for tops of pies.

7. On a floured surface, roll second disc of pie crust into a 12" square. Cut into strips of varying widths. Remove every other strip from square and weave them through remaining strips in the opposite direction to form a lattice. Gently press down on lattice to help hold it together. Cut lattice into seven 3" circles and transfer one circle to the top of each pie. Press around the edges of each pie to seal. Brush tops with reserved juice from filling and sprinkle with sugar.

8. Bake for 25 minutes, cover top of pan with foil to prevent over-browning, and bake an additional 20 minutes. Serve warm or cold. To easily remove pies from pan, run a thin-bladed knife around the inside of the cups.

10¼" Cast-Iron Skillet

TRIPLE-BERRY COBBLER

When I see my grandgirls come in from the garden, all rosy-cheeked and berry-stained, carrying buckets of strawberries, raspberries, and blueberries, I know I've done something right. Topped off with a serving of ice cream from one of my cows that my grandgirls helped milk the day before … well, it doesn't get any better than that.

MAKES: 6 SERVINGS

Berry Filling:

12	ozs strawberries, hulled and sliced (about 3 cups)
8	ozs raspberries (about 1½ cups)
4	ozs blueberries (about 1 cup)
¾	cup sugar
3	T cornstarch

Cobbler Topping:

1¼	cups flour
½	t baking powder
¼	t baking soda
¼	t salt
¼	cup butter
⅔	cup sugar
1	egg
½	t vanilla extract
¾	cup buttermilk

1. Preheat oven to 350°F.

2. In a large bowl, combine all ingredients for berry filling. Pour into a 10¼" cast-iron skillet; set aside.

3. Make topping: In a medium bowl, combine flour, baking powder, baking soda, and salt; set aside.

4. In a large bowl or stand mixer, blend butter and sugar until combined. Add egg and vanilla, blend until combined.

5. Add half of the flour mixture to the butter mixture; blend until combined. Add buttermilk; blend until combined. Add remaining flour mixture; blend until combined.

6. Pour batter over berries in skillet. Bake for 55–60 minutes, or until topping is golden brown and a toothpick inserted into the center comes out clean.

gluten free

Make it gluten free: Replace flour in recipe with 1 cup white rice flour and ¼ cup tapioca flour.

Cast-Iron Wedge Pan

Nectarine & Sour-Cream Wedge Cake

Aromatic summer stone fruits make such a lovely addition to baked goods, and thanks to my cast-iron wedge pan, I can bake up this nectarine-speckled cake in perfectly portioned slices. I love how the edges of each wedge turn out slightly crispy.

MAKES: 8 SERVINGS

Cake:

2	T butter, softened
$1/3$	cup sugar
$1/4$	cup sour cream
1	egg
$1/2$	t vanilla extract
$2/3$	cup flour
$1/4$	t baking soda
$1/4$	t baking powder
$1/8$	t salt
1	nectarine, peeled, pitted, and diced (about $1/2$ cup)

Icing:

2	T sour cream
$1/2$	cup powdered sugar

1. Preheat oven to 350°F. Butter a cast-iron wedge pan; set aside.

2. In a medium bowl or stand mixer, cream butter, sugar, and sour cream together. Add egg and vanilla; mix until blended, scraping bowl as needed.

3. In a small bowl, combine flour, baking soda, baking powder, and salt. Add to sour-cream mixture and mix until smooth.

4. Stir in diced nectarine and divide batter evenly among wedge pan cavities. Bake for 20–22 minutes, or until a toothpick inserted into the center comes out clean. Remove from oven and cool completely.

5. Once cake is cool, make icing: In a small bowl, combine sour cream and powdered sugar; mix until smooth. Evenly divide icing among cake wedges.

Make it gluten free: Replace flour in recipe with $1/3$ cup white rice flour and $1/4$ cup tapioca flour.

Cast-Iron Loaf Pan

½ cup butter, softened
1 cup sugar
2 eggs
¼ cup buttermilk
½ t vanilla extract
1¼ cups flour
¾ t baking soda
¼ t salt
⅛ t pulverized cardamom seeds
(about 1 pod)
½ lb plums, pitted and diced
(about 1 cup)

PLUM POUND CAKE

Classic pound cake is hard to beat, but the addition of tart-sweet plums and spicy-sweet cardamom makes it even better. My farm is home to many thriving plum trees, and in the early fall, we can't get enough of the prolific, sweet, juicy fruit the trees bear.

MAKES: 1 LOAF

1. Preheat oven to 350°F. Generously butter a cast-iron loaf pan.

2. In a large bowl or stand mixer, cream butter and sugar together. Add eggs one at a time, mixing well after each addition and scraping bowl as needed. Mix in buttermilk and vanilla.

3. In a medium bowl, combine flour, baking soda, salt, and cardamom. Add flour mixture to butter mixture and mix until smooth.

4. Add plums to batter and mix well. Add batter to prepared loaf pan. Bake for 55–60 minutes, or until a toothpick inserted into the center comes out clean.

Cast-Iron Mini-Cake Pan

Dough:

1½	cups flour, plus more for dusting
1	t baking powder
½	t baking soda
¼	t salt
1½	T brown sugar
4	T cold butter, cut into pieces
¾	cup buttermilk

Filling:

¾	cup pecans, chopped
⅓	cup brown sugar
2	T butter, melted
½	t cinnamon
½	t nutmeg

Maple Glaze:

1	T butter, melted
2	T maple syrup
⅓	cup powdered sugar
¼	cup pecans, chopped

MAPLE STICKY BUNS

You could consider these sticky buns a shortcut to cinnamon rolls. The quick buttermilk dough is dressed up with pecans, brown sugar, and spices. Then, it's rolled up jelly-roll style and cut into seven slices, each of which fits rather perfectly in my cast-iron mini-cake pan. After baking, they're topped with a rich, creamy maple glaze.

MAKES: 7 STICKY BUNS

1. Preheat oven to 425°F. Lightly butter cups of a cast-iron mini-cake pan.

2. Make dough: In a medium bowl, combine flour, baking powder, baking soda, salt, and brown sugar. Cut in butter using a pastry blender or fork until mixture resembles coarse crumbs. Add buttermilk and mix just until dough forms.

3. Dust a clean work surface with flour, place dough on surface, dust with more flour, and roll dough into a 12" x 15" rectangle.

4. Make filling: In a small bowl, combine pecans, brown sugar, butter, cinnamon, and nutmeg.

5. Spread filling over dough. Starting from a 12" side, roll dough up jellyroll style. Cut roll into 7 slices and place a slice in each prepared mini-cake pan cup.

6. Bake for 15–18 minutes, or until golden brown. Cool in pan for 30 minutes.

7. Make maple glaze: In a small bowl, combine melted butter, maple syrup, and powdered sugar; mix until smooth. Evenly divide glaze between sticky buns and sprinkle with chopped pecans. You may serve immediately, or wait for the glaze to firm up (about 15 minutes).

14" Cast-Iron Baking Pan

Dough:

1¼ cups buttermilk
1   T honey
¼   t salt
1   package active dry yeast
     (about 2¼ t)
2½   cups flour, plus more for dusting
1   egg

Cinnamon Sugar Filling:

½   cup butter, melted
1   cup sugar
4   t cinnamon

CINNAMON SUGAR KNOTS

Whenever my mom baked a pie, she would cut the extra dough into strips, dip them in cinnamon and sugar, twist them up, and bake them. This recipe embodies that same concept, only with soft, yeasted buttermilk dough.

MAKES: 8 KNOTS

1. Make dough: In a small saucepan, combine buttermilk, honey, and salt. Over medium-low heat, whisk mixture until honey is dissolved (mixture shouldn't feel hot on the inside of your wrist). Remove from heat, whisk in yeast, and set aside.

2. Add flour to a stand mixer fitted with a dough hook. Make a depression in the center of the flour to receive the liquid; add buttermilk mixture and egg to flour.

3. Mix until dough forms, and continue to mix until dough is smooth and pliable (5–8 minutes).

4. Lightly butter a medium bowl. Dust hands and dough with flour and shape into a ball (dough will be tacky). Place in prepared bowl, cover with plastic wrap, and let rise in a warm place for 1½ hours, or until doubled in bulk.

5. Prepare filling: Add melted butter to a small bowl. In a pie plate, combine sugar and cinnamon; set aside.

6. Preheat oven to 400°F. Lightly butter a 14" cast-iron griddle.

7. Divide dough into 8 portions. On a lightly floured surface, roll each portion into a 16"-long rope. Dip each rope in butter, and then dip in cinnamon-sugar mixture, turning to completely coat.

8. Fold rope in half; twist into a spiral. Roll spiral into a coiled circle and place on prepared griddle. Repeat with remaining ropes.

9. Bake for 15 minutes.

CRISPY SUGAR BOWLS

Okay, this is probably one of the more unique desserts I've ever tasted. One part sugar-ice-cream cone, and one part sundae, it speaks presentation, but it shouts, "Dig in!" Go ahead, pretend you're a kid again.

MAKES: 7 BOWLS

¼	cup sugar
1	egg
⅓	cup milk
3	T butter, melted
1	T molasses
¼	t vanilla extract
¼	cup flour

ice cream and toppings for serving

1. In a small bowl, combine sugar, egg, milk, butter, molasses, and vanilla.

2. Add flour and mix well. Let the batter rest for about 10 minutes, stirring occasionally.

3. Preheat a 10½" cast-iron griddle over medium-low heat. Add 2 T of batter to center of pan and evenly spread batter into a 6" circle. Cook for 3 minutes, flip over, and cover with a round cast-iron grill press. Cook for 2 minutes, remove press, flip over, and cook an additional 2 minutes, or until deep golden brown (if disc is not deep golden brown on both sides, continue flipping and cooking until both sides are evenly browned).

4. To shape discs into bowls, center a hot disc over a single cup in a cast-iron mini-cake pan and press into the cup with the bottom of a glass. Cool completely.

5. Repeat with remaining batter. Serve filled with ice cream, topped with your favorite toppings, or store in an airtight container for up to 3 days.

Cast-Iron Mini-Cake Pan

7½" Round Cast-Iron Grill Press

10½" Cast-Iron Griddle

180

14" Cast-Iron Baking Pan

Dough:

1 ²⁄₃	cups buttermilk
¼	cup honey
1	t salt
1	T active dry yeast
5	cups flour, plus more for dusting
2	eggs
4	T butter, softened and cut into pieces

Filling:

2	firm baking apples (like Granny Smith or Pink Lady), peeled, cored, and finely diced (about 3 cups)
4	T butter, cut into pieces
2	T honey
1	t cinnamon
½	t nutmeg

Caramel Sauce:

½	cup brown sugar
¼	cup sugar
2	T butter
½	cup heavy cream
¾	t salt
½	t vanilla extract

Vintage Cast-Iron Apple Peeler

CARAMEL-APPLE CINNAMON-ROLL WREATH

If you want to make a dessert that shouts, "Look at me, look at me!" this one is for you. Don't be deterred by the wreath concept—it's actually quite easy to shape. After spreading filling over the dough and rolling it, bring the two ends together to form a ring. Then, cut the top of the ring into slices while leaving the back of the ring intact, turn the slices 90°, and voila—a wreath!

MAKES: 16–18 CINNAMON ROLLS

1. Make dough: In a medium saucepan over low heat, combine buttermilk, honey, and salt. Cook just until warm and honey is dissolved (mixture shouldn't feel hot on the inside of your wrist). Remove from heat, whisk in yeast, and let stand until frothy (about 5 minutes).

2. Meanwhile, add flour and eggs to a stand mixer fitted with a dough hook. Add yeast mixture and mix well. With mixer running, add butter, one piece at a time. Knead for 5–8 minutes, until dough is smooth and elastic. Place in a bowl, cover with plastic wrap, and let rise in a warm place for 1½ hours.

3. Prepare filling: In a medium skillet over medium heat, combine apples, butter, and honey. Cook until apples are soft (about 12 minutes); mix in cinnamon and nutmeg.

4. Preheat oven to 400°F. Generously butter a round 14" cast-iron baking pan.

5. After dough has risen, press down to deflate. Dust a clean work surface with flour and roll dough into a 16" x 20" rectangle; spread filling over dough. Beginning from the longest edge, roll dough up into a cylinder.

6. Transfer cylinder to prepared baking pan and form into a ring, joining the two ends together. Using kitchen shears, cut dough into 1½"-thick slices, while leaving the ring intact in the back. After the ring has been cut, turn the pieces upward to see the inner rings of the cinnamon roll. Cover with plastic wrap and let rise for 30 minutes. After rising, remove plastic wrap and bake for 25 minutes, or until light golden brown.

7. Prepare caramel sauce: In a medium cast-iron skillet over medium-low heat, combine sugars. Whisking frequently, cook until sugar melts (this should start happening within 5 minutes, but watch closely so it doesn't burn).

8. Once sugar is melted, add butter and whisk until melted. Whisk in cream, salt, and vanilla. Cool slightly and serve with cinnamon roll wreath.

8" Cast-Iron Skillet

Crust:

Medium Butter Cookie Pie Crust,
p. 186

Filling:

12	ozs strawberries, hulled and quartered (about 3 cups)
8	ozs rhubarb, thickly sliced (about 2 cups)
1¾	cups water
⅓	cup sugar
1	t MaryJane's ChillOver Powder (MaryJanesFarm.org)

Italian Meringue:

⅔	cup sugar
⅓	cup water
3	egg whites, at room temperature
¼	t cream of tartar
¼	t salt

STRAWBERRY RHUBARB PIE WITH ITALIAN MERINGUE

Have you ever made a meringue pie and baked it to golden-brown perfection, only to find that the center is still gooey? I've been there. The beauty of Italian meringue is that, since you drizzle hot syrup into the egg whites, they're partially cooked *before* they go into the oven, reducing the chance that you'll have a troublesome meringue on your hands.

MAKES: ONE 8" PIE

1. Make Medium Butter Cookie Pie Crust, as directed on p. 186.

2. Preheat oven to 400°F. Lightly butter an 8" cast-iron skillet.

3. Roll pie crust out onto a lightly floured surface; let rest for 5 minutes (helps prevent crust from slipping and shrinking while baking). Transfer to prepared skillet. Poke holes in the bottom of crust with a fork, line with foil, add pie weights, and bake for 20 minutes. Cool while making filling.

4. Make filling: In a large saucepan over medium heat, bring strawberries, rhubarb, and water to a boil; simmer for 10 minutes. Strain the juice and discard pulp. You should have 2 cups juice (if you have less, add water to make 2 cups).

5. In a medium saucepan over medium heat, bring juice and sugar to a boil. Whisk in ChillOver powder, boil an additional 3 minutes; cool slightly, and pour into baked pie crust. Cool until set, about 2 hours, or overnight.

6. Preheat oven to 375°F.

7. Make meringue: In a small saucepan over medium heat, combine sugar and water, stirring just until sugar is dissolved. Without stirring, cook until syrup reaches 240°F on a candy thermometer.

8. Meanwhile, whip egg whites until foamy. Add cream of tartar and salt; whip egg whites into soft peaks. While mixing, pour syrup into egg whites in a slow, steady stream. Once all syrup is added, whip into stiff, glossy peaks.

9. Spoon meringue onto pie and form into desired shape; bake for 10–12 minutes, or until golden. Cool completely and serve.

BUTTER-COOKIE PIE CRUST

Over the years, I've learned that there's a particular finesse to working with pie crust. Contrary to my original views, it takes a firm hand to shape a pie crust and bend it to your will. Not only that, but while most pie-crust recipes have similar ingredients, they're not equal. The right balance between fat, flour, and moisture produces the perfect pie crust.

MAKES: ONE CRUST

Small Pie Crust:

1¼	cups flour
½	t sugar
¼	t salt
½	cup cold butter, cut into pieces
2½	T cold water

Medium Pie Crust:

1¾	cups flour
¾	t sugar
¼	t salt
10	T cold butter, cut into pieces
¼	cup cold water

Large Pie Crust:

2½	cups flour
1	t sugar
½	t salt
1	cup cold butter, cut into pieces
5	T cold water

Note: This recipe is for pie crust only. For complete rolling and baking instructions, see Mini Apple Pies on p. 168, Rhubarb Raspberry Pandowdy on p. 187, or Strawberry Rhubarb Pie on p. 184.

1. Combine flour, sugar, and salt in a food processor. Cut in butter until mixture resembles coarse meal. With food processor running, slowly add water. Shape into one disc if making recipe for small or medium crusts and two discs if making recipe for large crust. Wrap in plastic wrap, and chill for 1 hour, and then use in desired recipe.

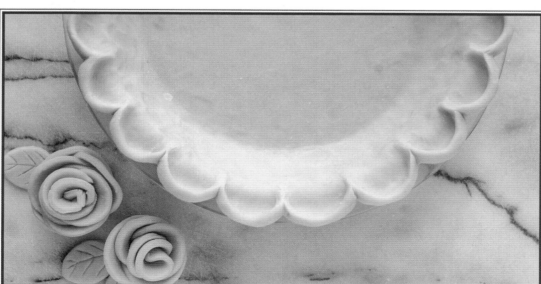

RHUBARB RASPBERRY PANDOWDY

Pandowdy is an early American cooked fruit dish with a biscuit or pie-crust top, originally eaten for breakfast because it was easily cooked on hot coals left over from the night before. It was most commonly made with apples, but the recipe passed down by word of mouth using whatever ingredients were available or common to an area.

MAKES: 8 SERVINGS

1. Make Medium Butter Cookie Pie Crust, as directed on p. 186.

2. Preheat oven to 400°F.

3. Combine all filling ingredients except butter in a large bowl and toss until fruit is coated. Put fruit into a buttered 10¼" cast-iron skillet. Dot with butter.

4. Roll pie crust out onto a lightly floured surface and transfer to skillet. Tuck the edges of dough in, pressing on the fruit.

5. Bake for 30 minutes. Reduce heat to 350°F and continue to bake for 15 more minutes. Pull the skillet out and slice the pie crust into squares (like you would a bar cookie), and return skillet to oven for 10 more minutes. The crust then submerges partially into the fruit juices—the trademark of a 'pandowdy'! Serve warm by the big spoonful with some freshly whipped cream or a scoop of vanilla ice cream.

10¼" Cast-Iron Skillet

Crust:

Medium Butter Cookie Pie Crust, p. 186

Filling:

1	lb raspberries, fresh or frozen, but not thawed (about 3 cups)
2	cups rhubarb, finely chopped
¾	cup sugar
¼	cup flour
½	t cinnamon
¼	t grated nutmeg
¼	t salt
2	T butter, cut into pieces

whipped cream or vanilla ice cream for serving

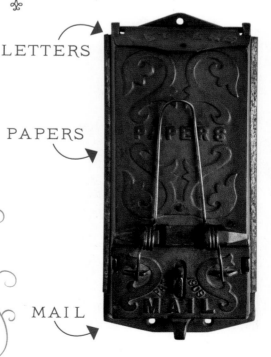

LETTERS

PAPERS

MAIL

8" Cast-Iron Skillet

²/₃ cup white rice flour
½ cup cocoa powder
½ t baking powder
¼ t salt
1 cup sugar
½ cup butter
½ cup semi-sweet chocolate chips
2 eggs
2 t vanilla extract
¼ cup peanut butter
1 T powdered sugar

Special Equipment:

pastry bag
Wilton #7 round piping tip

PEANUT-BUTTER SKILLET BROWNIES

There are two qualities I think every brownie should have: a rich, moist, chocolate center and a chewy, slightly crisp edge. This brownie recipe has both, and the peanut-butter topping is a wonderful addition. Enjoy with a cold glass of milk.

MAKES: 8 SERVINGS

1. Preheat oven to 350°F. Lightly butter an 8" cast-iron skillet.

2. In a medium bowl, combine rice flour, cocoa powder, baking powder, and salt; mix in sugar and set aside.

3. In a medium saucepan over medium-low heat, melt butter and chocolate together, whisking frequently. Once melted, remove from heat and whisk in eggs and vanilla.

4. Add flour mixture to chocolate mixture and mix well. Pour into prepared skillet, smooth out top, and set aside.

5. In a small bowl, combine peanut butter and powdered sugar. Spoon into a pastry bag fitted with a Wilton #7 round piping tip. Make several rings of peanut butter mixture over the brownie batter. With the tip of a toothpick or a thin-bladed knife, make four lines in the peanut butter, starting from the outer edge and moving toward the center. Make four lines in between the first four, this time starting in the center and moving toward the edge.

6. Bake for 35–40 minutes, or until a toothpick inserted into the center comes out clean. Cool completely and enjoy!

10½" Cast-Iron Griddle

Cookie:

1	cup flour
¼	t baking powder
¼	t baking soda
¼	t salt
1½	t ground ginger
½	cup butter, softened
¼	cup sugar
¼	cup dark brown sugar
1	egg
1	T molasses
1	t vanilla extract

Icing:

⅔	cup powdered sugar
5	t milk

GRIDDLE GINGER COOKIE

My multi-purpose cast-iron griddle makes a mean cookie. After baking and cooling, this cookie slices up into moist, chewy, delicious cookie wedges.

MAKES: ONE 10½" COOKIE

1. Preheat oven to 325°F. Generously butter a 10½" cast-iron griddle.

2. Make cookie: In a small bowl, combine flour, baking powder, baking soda, salt, and ground ginger; set aside.

3. In a medium bowl or stand mixer, cream butter, sugar, and brown sugar together, scraping bowl occasionally. Add egg, molasses, and vanilla; continue mixing until smooth.

4. Add flour mixture to butter mixture and mix until smooth. Spoon mixture onto prepared griddle pan. Lightly butter hands and flatten mixture so that it touches the edges of the pan. Bake cookie for 25 minutes. Cool completely in pan.

5. Once cookie is cool, prepare icing: In a small bowl, combine powdered sugar and milk; mix until smooth. Drizzle mixture over center of cookie. Using the back of a spoon, spread icing out in a smooth layer. Let dry for 10 minutes and enjoy.

gluten free

Make it gluten free: Replace flour in recipe with ⅔ cup white rice flour, ⅓ cup tapioca flour, and ½ t xanthan gum.

36-oz Cast-Iron Oval Serving Dish

BAKED PEACHES

These baked peaches are proof that there's beauty in simplicity. For an easy summer dessert, just mix up a little crumb topping, spoon onto halved peaches, and bake. Be sure to top it all off with a scoop of vanilla ice cream.

MAKES: 6 SERVINGS

3   peaches, halved and pitted
¼   cup flour
2   T thick-cut rolled oats
2   T brown sugar
2   T butter, melted
vanilla ice cream for serving

1. Preheat oven to 350°F.

2. Arrange peaches cut side up in cast-iron baking dish.

3. In a small bowl, combine flour, oats, and brown sugar; mix in melted butter.

4. Evenly divide oat mixture among peaches. Bake for 25–30 minutes, until oat mixture is golden brown and peaches are tender. Cool slightly and serve with vanilla ice cream.

BAKED CHURROS

Craving something sweet, but short on time? These churros are ready to satisfy your sweet tooth without making you wait in hungry anticipation.

MAKES: 24 CHURROS

15" x 12¼" Cast-Iron Rectangular Griddle

Churros:

2	cups flour, plus more for dusting
1½	t baking powder
½	t baking soda
½	t salt
¼	cup butter, softened
2	T honey
1	egg
½	t vanilla extract
½	cup milk

Topping:

½	cup sugar
2	t cinnamon
3	T butter, melted

1. Preheat oven to 400°F.

2. Make churros: In a small bowl, combine flour, baking powder, baking soda, and salt; set aside. In a medium bowl or stand mixer, blend butter and honey until combined. Add egg and vanilla; mix well.

3. Alternately add the flour mixture and milk to the butter mixture, beginning and ending with flour.

4. Dust a clean surface with flour and roll dough to ⅛" thickness. Cut dough into 1" x 8" strips, twist each to form a spiral, and place on a 15" x 12¼" cast-iron griddle (you will be able to fit about 8 churros on the griddle at a time). Bake for 8–10 minutes, or until churros start to turn golden brown.

5. Make topping: While churros are baking, combine sugar and cinnamon in a small bowl. Pour onto a plate and set aside.

6. Remove churros from oven, brush with butter, and roll in cinnamon and sugar mixture. Repeat process with remaining dough.

8" Cast-Iron Skillet

1¼ cups bittersweet chocolate
chips (about 8 ozs)
¼ cup peanut butter
8 ozs marshmallows, cut into ½"
cubes (about 2 cups)
(for our homemade recipe, see
RaisingJane.org/journal/57468)
graham crackers for serving

SKILLET S'MORES

S'mores without a campfire, you ask? Why, of course! The steady heat of your cast-iron skillet is just what you need to make delicious, gooey s'mores right in your oven, even in the middle of winter, if you're so inclined.

MAKES: 8 SERVINGS

1. Preheat oven to 400°F.

2. Add chocolate chips to an 8" cast-iron skillet. Spoon peanut butter over chocolate chips and top with marshmallows.

3. Bake for 10 minutes, then turn broiler on to toast tops of marshmallows. Serve with graham crackers.

6-Cavity Cast-Iron Muffin Pan

LUEBERRY MUFFINS WITH COCONUT LEMON TOPPING

I often feel that muffins are cupcakes masquerading as something a little more healthful. With that being said, this combination of blueberries, coconut, and lemon makes me a little weak in the knees. Let's just say I've eaten more than my fair share of these muffins.

MAKES: 6 MUFFINS

Coconut Lemon Topping:

⅓ cup flour
¼ cup finely shredded coconut
¼ cup honey crystals
3 T butter, softened
1 T lemon zest
⅛ t salt

Blueberry-Muffin Batter:

¾ cup flour
½ t baking powder
¼ t baking soda
⅛ t salt
¼ cup butter, softened
½ cup honey crystals
1 egg
1 t vanilla extract
⅓ cup milk
3 ozs fresh or frozen blueberries
(about ¾ cup)

1. Make topping: combine all ingredients in a medium bowl, and blend with a pastry blender until mixture resembles coarse crumbs; set aside.

2. Preheat oven to 400°F. Lightly butter a 6-cavity cast-iron muffin pan.

3. Make muffin batter: In a small bowl, combine flour, baking powder, baking soda, and salt; set aside. In a medium bowl or stand mixer, beat butter and honey crystals until smooth. Add egg and vanilla; mix well.

4. Add about half of the flour mixture to butter mixture and mix well. Add milk and mix well. Add remaining flour and mix well. Stir in blueberries.

5. Divide batter evenly between muffin cups, then divide topping evenly between muffin cups.

6. Bake for 15 minutes, cover with aluminum foil (to prevent topping from burning), and bake an additional 15–20 minutes, or until a toothpick inserted into the center of a muffin comes out clean.

8" Cast-Iron Skillet

Bread-Pudding Apples:

¼ cup sugar
1 t cornstarch
1½ cups milk
2 egg yolks, whisked
½ t vanilla extract
4 cups ½" brioche bread cubes
   (crusts removed)
2 T butter, melted
½ t cinnamon
2 T raisins
4 Granny Smith apples
1 lemon wedge

Caramel Sauce:

6 T butter
¼ cup maple syrup
¼ cup brown sugar
¼ t vanilla extract
2 T heavy cream

BAKED BREAD-PUDDING APPLES

Maybe I'm alone in this, but I've always considered bread pudding to be an incomplete dessert. I need a dessert with texture and substance, and bread pudding always fell short. But hollowed-out apples stuffed with bread pudding and topped with caramel sauce? I'm in!

MAKES: 4 APPLES

1. Preheat oven to 350°F.

2. Make filling: In a medium saucepan, combine sugar and cornstarch; whisk in milk. Cook over medium heat just until steam rises from the milk. Pour a little hot milk into the whisked egg yolks to temper, then pour egg yolks into the saucepan, whisking well. Cook over medium-low heat until thickened (about 3 minutes). Remove custard from heat, stir in vanilla, and set aside.

3. Add bread cubes to a medium bowl. Add butter, cinnamon, and raisins. Toss to combine and set aside.

4. Cut off the tops of the apples and rub with a lemon wedge. Draw a circle ¼" from the edge of the apple with the tip of a knife. Using the drawn circle as a guide, hollow out each apple with a melon baller, leaving about ¼" of thickness at the bottom. Arrange apples in an 8" cast-iron skillet.

5. Combine the bread cubes and custard and spoon mixture into each apple, piling the filling up at the top. Bake for 20 minutes, or until the apples are fork-tender.

6. Make caramel sauce: In a small saucepan, combine butter, maple syrup, and brown sugar. Bring to a simmer over medium heat, stirring constantly. Simmer for 2 minutes; remove from heat. Stir in vanilla and cream. Serve over baked apples.

10¼" Cast-Iron Skillet

Crust:

¾ cup pecans
1 cup flour, plus more for dusting
¼ cup brown sugar
¼ t salt
½ cup cold butter, cut into pieces
3 T cold water

Filling:

2 sweet potatoes, peeled and cooked
½ cup milk
½ cup butter, melted
3 eggs
¾ cup brown sugar
1 t vanilla extract
1 t cinnamon
¼ t nutmeg

Caramel Pecan Topping:

4 T butter
¼ cup brown sugar
¼ cup maple syrup
½ cup pecans, chopped
½ t vanilla extract

PECAN CRUST SWEET-POTATO PIE

Every Thanksgiving, my son, Brian, enthusiastically requests this pie. In fact, he often makes it himself and proudly comes to dinner bearing his creation. The pecan crust is wonderful with the filling, but it can be a bit soft and fragile. As you work, don't be afraid to dust with extra flour as needed.

MAKES: ONE 10¼" PIE

1. Make crust: Add pecans, flour, sugar, and salt to a food processor; pulse until pecans are ground. Add butter and pulse until mixture resembles coarse crumbs. Sprinkle in water; pulse until dough forms. Wrap in plastic wrap and chill for 45 minutes.

2. Preheat oven to 375°F.

3. Roll dough out onto a lightly floured surface and transfer to a 10¼" cast-iron skillet. Line crust with foil, weigh down with pie weights, and bake for 12 minutes.

4. Make filling: Add all filling ingredients to a food processor and pulse until smooth. Pour filling into crust and bake for 50 minutes. Let pie cool for 50 minutes or chill overnight, then prepare caramel.

5. Make topping: In a small saucepan over medium heat, combine butter, sugar, and syrup. Stirring frequently, bring to a simmer. Stop stirring and continue to simmer for 3 minutes. Mix in pecans and vanilla. Serve warm over pie.

2-qt Cast-Iron Saucepan

6   T butter
2   cups white chocolate chips
2   T almond butter
1   T honey
1½ cups thick-rolled oats,
    gluten-free
¼   cup sliced almonds, chopped
¼   t almond extract
⅓   cup apricot preserves

gluten free

No-Bake Apricot Almond Thumbprints

No recipe arsenal would be complete without a great no-bake cookie recipe. And do I have a recipe for you! The oats, white chocolate, and apricot preserves are amazing together. I dare you to eat just one.

MAKES: 24 COOKIES

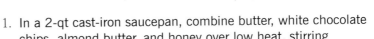

1. In a 2-qt cast-iron saucepan, combine butter, white chocolate chips, almond butter, and honey over low heat, stirring constantly. Once all ingredients are melted together, stir in oats, almonds, and almond extract.

2. Drop tablespoonfuls of mixture onto wax paper and shape into discs, creating a depression in the center of each.

3. Spoon apricot preserves into the depressions, and cool for 30 minutes.

Enameled Cast-Iron Mini
Round Cocotte
(Note: these recipes call for 4 cocottes)

Raspberry Lemon Crisp:
Crumb Topping:

1	cup flour
1	T lemon zest
1/3	cup sugar
2	T lemon juice (about 1 lemon)
3	T butter, melted

Filling:

1¼	lbs fresh raspberries (about 3¾ cups)
3	T cornstarch
1	cup sugar
¼	cup fresh lemon juice (about 2 lemons)

Pineapple Blueberry Cobbler:
Topping:

¾	cup flour
¼	t salt
½	t baking powder
½	cup sour cream
½	cup sugar
1	egg
¼	cup milk
2	ozs fresh blueberries (about ½ cup)

Filling:

2	cups pineapple, cut into tidbits
1	cup blueberries
2	t cornstarch
½	cup brown sugar

RASPBERRY LEMON SINGLE-SERVE CRISP

The first time I tasted a crisp, I thought it was the best dessert I'd ever had. I marveled at the crumbly topping and thought that it surely had to be complicated to make. Once I started to tinker in the kitchen and figured out just how easy it was to whip up a crumb topping, I was positively delighted.

MAKES: 4 MINI CRISPS

1. Preheat oven to 375°F. Lightly butter four enameled cast-iron mini round cocottes. Line a large baking sheet with parchment paper.

2. Make topping: In a medium bowl, combine all topping ingredients.

3. Make filling: In a medium saucepan, combine all filling ingredients. Cook over medium heat, stirring occasionally, until thickened.

4. Divide filling evenly between prepared cocottes; top with crumb topping.

5. Place cocottes on a large baking sheet and bake for 25–30 minutes, or until topping is golden brown.

PINEAPPLE BLUEBERRY SINGLE-SERVE COBBLER

MAKES: 4 MINI COBBLERS

1. Preheat oven to 350°F. Lightly butter four enameled cast-iron mini round cocottes.

2. Make topping: In a small bowl, combine flour, salt, and baking powder. In a medium bowl, combine sour cream, sugar, and egg. Pour a portion of the flour mixture into the sour cream mixture, then add a little milk, alternating until all have been combined.

3. Make filling: Combine filling ingredients in a medium bowl. Divide filling evenly among cocottes; top with the batter. Press remaining blueberries into the batter.

4. Place cocottes on a large baking sheet and bake for 25–30 minutes, or until a toothpick inserted into the center of one of the cobblers comes out clean.

Raspberry Lemon Crisp

10¼" Cast-Iron Skillet

Biscuits:

1   half batch Buttermilk Biscuits, p. 88

Apple Pie:

½   cup brown sugar
2   t cinnamon
½   t nutmeg
¼   t ginger
6   T butter, melted
1   qt Apple Pie Filling (p. 209)
⅓   cup pecans, finely chopped
whipped cream for serving (optional)

 UTTERMILK-BISCUIT APPLE PIE

This recipe came to me shortly after my daughter, Meg, gave me a jar of her homemade apple-pie filling for Christmas. I wondered what would happen if I made a mess of buttermilk biscuits, placed them in my cast-iron skillet, and poured the pie filling over the whole thing. My biggest question as I watched the pie bake was if the biscuits would cook through. I pulled it out of the oven, and lo and behold, the biscuits were cooked to perfection.

MAKES: 6 SERVINGS

1. Preheat oven to 375°F. Generously butter a 10¼" cast-iron skillet.

2. Prep a half batch of Buttermilk-Biscuit dough, p. 88. Set aside after cutting six 3" biscuits from the dough.

3. In a shallow bowl or pie plate, combine brown sugar, cinnamon, nutmeg, and ginger. Dip each unbaked biscuit in butter and coat in brown sugar mixture. Arrange biscuits in bottom of prepared skillet.

4. Pour Apple-Pie Filling over biscuits. Add pecans to remaining sugar mixture and spread evenly over apple pie filling.

5. Place skillet on a large baking sheet and bake for 40–45 minutes. Cool slightly and serve warm. If desired, top with whipped cream.

 ## Apple-Pie Filling

18	lbs (approx.) apples such as Cameo, Gala, Winesap, Braeburn, or Jonagold
4½	cups sugar
1	cup corn or rice starch
2	T ground cinnamon
1	t salt
½	t ground nutmeg
10	cups water
6	T fresh lemon juice (about 3 lemons), divided

1. Wash apples, then peel, core, and slice. As you work, fill three large bowls with apples. Fill each bowl with enough cold water to cover. Add 1 T lemon juice per bowl to prevent them from browning.

2. In a large pot, combine sugar, starch, cinnamon, salt, nutmeg, and water. Bring to a boil, stirring constantly for approximately 15 minutes or until thick and caramel-colored. Remove from heat and stir in remaining 3 T lemon juice.

3. Ladle apples into sterilized quart jars. Ladle the hot liquid over the apples leaving ½" headspace. Refer to a canning manual for complete canning instructions.

MAKES: SEVEN QUART JARS

Cast-Iron Restoration & Maintenance

Both vintage and newly-manufactured-but-neglected cast iron can be brought back to life with a little TLC.

Depending on the date of its manufacture, the surface texture should be uniformly smooth (the actual metal). If you see what some people refer to as "a surface that is flaking off," the piece can be easily renewed because the only thing flaking off is a buildup of the layers and layers of bad oil crusted on from misuse.

All the piece needs from you is to be properly re-seasoned, also referred to as "cured," or in technical terms, its surface needs several applications of oil that you heat just right until it becomes polymerized, forming a thin layer of hardened "shellac" that you can barely see—cast iron's version of a non-stick surface.

If it's a newer piece (not so very vintage), its metal surface will most likely be rough (like a cat's tongue).

If it's a vintage piece, it will probably have a smoother surface. On this vintage piece, you can see some of the circular machining from when it was manufactured—not a problem as far as cooking goes because even though it looks grooved, it feels smooth to the touch.

new

vintage

Unless cast iron is manufactured on a small scale, modern manufacturing techniques are different than they used to be, but that doesn't mean you can't love a newly manufactured piece. I have both old and new. Now that I have my daily cast-iron maintenance down to a science, and I've figured out how to cure a mistreated piece (the polymerized thing), they're all the same to me.

If you're wondering about the vintage pieces that readily show up in secondhand stores or online stores like eBay, avoid pieces that are deeply pitted, chipped, cracked, deeply scratched, or warped (this is important!).

chipped

cracked

By warped, I mean it isn't flat on the bottom. If it's warped on the bottom, it won't sit flat on your stove. That's particularly problematic if you're cooking on a ceramic stovetop. Not only will it make your heating element work overtime, the piece is likely to scoot around on your stovetop or your counter whenever you're stirring food, potentially scratching their surfaces.

Warping is usually a result of someone tossing the entire piece into a raging campfire (not the softly glowing coals needed for cooking with cast-iron on a campfire) while saying to themselves, "Now, I won't have a skillet sitting around looking neglected—fresh start, here I come." Unfortunately, campfire flames range anywhere from 1,100°F (dark-red flames) to 2,000°F (orange-yellow flames) and can cause warping of the metal. Or perhaps the piece was super-hot and then splashed with cold water. Can you put your piece in your modern oven and set the dial for self-cleaning? Yes, you can!!!! That temperature is around 900 to 1,000°F. More on that in a minute.

Okay, let's get this do-over restoration thing out of the way first, because once you understand how to give cast iron a fresh start, daily maintenance will make more sense. Again, if you bring home a piece that is "flaking" and/or merely rusty without any of the fatal flaws I mentioned above, it's time for a strip-down makeover.

STRIPPING CAST IRON

If you have a modern oven with a self-cleaning cycle and an exhaust fan, you can let it do most of the work so that when you scrub your piece down using one of my methods on the next page, it'll only take a few minutes. Put your cast-iron piece in your modern oven (or make friends with someone who does have one), and set the oven on its clean cycle. You can't do this if your piece has wooden or Bakelite handles, although sometimes, they can be easily removed.

(continued)

The little skillet in this set fries an egg like a dream. A sunny-side-up egg slides right out and onto a plate.

(continued from p. 211)

SCRUBBING by HAND:

When it comes to cast-iron restoration, your new best friend is 220-grit drywall sanding screen made by 3M. This stuff is the bomb for cast iron. Cut it into smaller pieces, put on a pair of gloves, and be amazed at how quickly it does the job. Plus, you can rinse the screen off as you work and it's good to go again. No need to push too hard—it's best to "handle with care."

SCRUBBING with DRILL & BRUSH:

Get yourself gloved and goggled up (make sure you don't have loose-fitting clothing on, and if you have long hair, make sure it's up and out of the way) and use a power drill with a brush attached to remove old layers of oil or rust. You'll need a crimped wire-cup steel brush. I like a 1½" brush, but a 2" brush also works. If managing the drill with one hand while holding your piece steady with the other is a problem for you, try putting the piece in a table vise (padded with a rag) so you can hold the drill with two hands.

Or, you can use a Dremel outfitted with a smaller brush. It's the same idea, except using a Dremel will take you a tad longer (not much, though—it goes pretty fast) and you might need more than one brush, depending on the shape your piece is in. You'll need a ½" carbon (cup-shaped) steel brush. The cup shape works on flat surfaces like the bottom of a skillet as well as when you "walk it up" the sides of pans.

Be sure to wear safety goggles while working on any project that could result in eye injury. Elvex Safety with Style has a line of safety glasses that are not only safe, but stylish, Elvex.com.

No, I don't recommend filling the pan with ammonia and setting it for seven days inside a black plastic bag outside in the hot sun or indoors next to a radiator. And no, I don't recommend an application of oven cleaner. Or a lye bath. Or muriatic acid. If you go that route, make sure you put on a hazmat suit and check to make sure you have good health insurance.

Now, wash your cast-iron piece in hot, soapy water using the scrubby side of a sponge. Give it a good scrub. Use plenty of soap this one time only, because once your piece is cured, you don't want to use soap very often, if at all, because it will slowly break down the polymerized surface you're about to give it by following the steps below. And then, MAINTAIN. That's right, the word maintain is all in CAPS for a reason.

Rinse and dry completely. It will probably still have some red rust tones to it, but as long as all surface "dust" has been washed off and a paper towel comes away clean, it's in good shape and ready to be cured.

Now, you're going to give it a polymerized "cured" surface. You'll need the following: paper towels and organic virgin coconut oil—I use Nutiva (read about curing oils on the next page). Extreme-heat gloves are optional but highly recommended.

1. Preheat your oven to 200°F.
2. Using paper towels, rub a VERY thin layer of coconut oil over the entire piece, both inside and outside.
3. Put it in the oven for 10 minutes.
4. Bring it back out (heat gloves recommended from here on out).
5. Crank your oven up to 365°F and turn on your exhaust fan.
6. While your oven is getting up to temperature, rub the entire piece again using paper towels, but DO NOT apply more coconut oil. You'll think you're wiping all the oil off, but you can't. Trust me. If you have so much on it that it looks oily, it'll pool up when heated. Even if you put your pan upside down in the oven, the surface of your piece might end up looking like mitochondrial DNA. Plus, you want to keep your oven and racks free from dripping oil, and if you do this step right, your oven will remain sparkling clean. You do have a clean oven, right?:)
7. Now, let it bake at 365°F for 20 minutes.
8. Turn your oven off and wait until your piece stops smoking before taking it from the oven and setting it on the top of your stove. Let your piece continue to cool down.
9. Turn your oven back on to 365°F. Wipe on another super-thin layer of coconut oil using a paper towel. With a clean towel, wipe it again without adding additional oil as if you were trying to wipe off the layer of oil you just applied.

Repeat steps 7 through 9 at least three times (four times total). After each session in your oven, your cast-iron piece will discolor a paper towel less and less until finally, your paper towel will come away clean.

first heat cycle  last heat cycle

Keep in mind, you don't need to do all the heat cycles on the same day. However, after you've rinsed and dried your piece right after stripping it, you'll want to run it through at least one heat cycle so it doesn't begin to rust. Also, if after your first heat cycle, you didn't trust me and realize you didn't get enough of the oil off and you have a few mitochondrial cells showing up, let your piece cool down completely, and take them off using either some fine-grit sandpaper or steel wool. Now is the time to make any course corrections.

(continued)

(continued from p. 213)

Start using your piece for light-duty foods (toast and pancakes rather than scrambled eggs), because every time you use it and then clean it properly, its surface will improve. Eat more bacon. It's no coincidence that old-timers tell us to "sear meat often" when it comes to maintaining the "cure" on cast iron.

If you're wondering about the science behind my method, it goes something like this. There are two things that matter about the oil you use: smoke point and purity. (Smoke point can correspond with the type of fatty acids in an oil, but let's not get sidetracked.) You want an oil above a certain smoke point (but not so high it puts most ovens out of the running). To produce an oil with a high smoke point, some manufacturers use techniques like bleaching, filtering, and heating to extract the compounds (minerals, enzymes, etc.) that don't play well with heat. The oil you use needs to be pure and simple. Additives do weird things to your health as well as to the surface of your cast-iron piece.

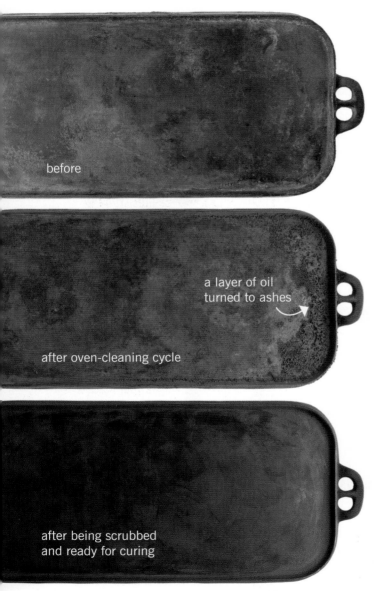

before

a layer of oil
turned to ashes

after oven-cleaning cycle

after being scrubbed
and ready for curing

Nutiva lists its ingredients as "organic, unrefined, cold-pressed virgin coconut oil." That's it, nothing else. Coconut oil is naturally semi-solid and requires no hydrogenation, plus it's missing ingredients like TBHO (whatever that is), and the monoglycerides and diglycerides found in most shortenings. And these days, shortening's once-pure predecessor, lard (pork fat), can have things like BHA, BHT, and propyl gallate added to it if it isn't organic. Nutiva coconut oil has a smoke point of 350°F. The smoke point is the temperature at which it begins to break down into glycerol and free fatty acids (the polymerized thing) and produce smoke. The reason smoke points are almost always included on labels is because the changes that happen to the oil (and the ensuing smoke) aren't good for us.

For many years, I used organic lard, but ever since I discovered organic virgin coconut oil, I've kept a small jar handy for all things cast iron. But, because people promote so many different oils for seasoning cast iron, I decided it would be good for me to test the cast-iron seasoning oils most commonly mentioned online. So, I completely stripped a large vintage griddle using the self-cleaning cycle on my range.

I divided my ready-to-be-cured griddle up into eight imaginary squares and tried the following organic oils using my curing method.

Flax Oil 225°F smoke point	**Olive Oil (virgin)** 320°F smoke point	**Coconut Oil (virgin)** 350°F smoke point	**Lard** 370°F smoke point	**Canola Oil** 425°F smoke point	**Peanut Oil** 450°F smoke point	**Shortening (Spectrum)** 450°F smoke point	**Sunflower Oil (high-oleic)** 460°F smoke point

After running my griddle through three heat cycles using the eight different oils, I did the first thing I always do to check to make sure the cure worked: I fried an egg, eight of them, to be exact. Several of them stuck horribly (flax, olive, canola, and sunflower). Lard was so-so. But coconut oil, Spectrum shortening, and peanut oil were clearly the winners. I continued to test curing oils on dozens of different skillets that I'd stripped in my oven. (I have close to 100 different cookware pieces I've collected over the years.) Meanwhile, I tested the eight different oils on my griddle for long-term durability by using it to cook pancakes and toast (using butter), then hamburgers and sausage patties (using safflower oil), and a vegetable stir-fry (using olive oil). Each time, after using it, I cleaned it with warm water, dried it, and then lightly coated the eight sections again with their appointed oils. Then, I fried eight eggs again to see how well the eight different types of oils were holding up. This time, the hands-down winner was virgin coconut oil. Neither side of a fried egg (that I flipped) was stuck to the pan one iota. I continued to test virgin coconut oil on both old and new cast iron skillets that I'd stripped first. Every time, an egg did not stick. Surprisingly, coconut oil doesn't work all that great when prepping pans for baked goods, even though it works perfect for curing cast iron.

Unlike liquid oils that are kept in dark bottles or cans in an attempt to keep them from going rancid (if a spot of oil on your tongue tastes bitter, it's gone rancid), coconut oil is extremely shelf-stable. In fact, if you buy a small jar (available on Amazon.com), you can put most of it into your freezer or refrigerator, enabling you to use it for what seems like forever for cast-iron restoration (all those gems you've brought home but haven't done anything with yet). For routine maintenance, I keep a small wide-mouth canning jar full of coconut oil on my counter next to my stove. Dipping your paper towel into a tub of white oil (solid at room temperature—liquid at 76°F) to grab a dab is a whole lot easier and less messy than tipping a glass bottle upside down every time you need a smidgen of oil.

As I pondered the different oils people use for curing cast iron, I wondered if people complain about durability issues with flax oil because of its low smoke point. And since flax oil is never recommended as a cooking oil, why would I put it on my cast-iron pans? Safflower oil has a smoke point of 510°F, which is a good thing, but how many people have an oven that will go to 525°F in order to use it as a curing oil? Peanut oil has the same smoke point as Spectrum shortening, 450°F, but it's a notorious allergen, even if technically, a highly refined oil doesn't carry the protein needed to cause an allergic reaction. I'll bet if you're allergic to peanuts, you're not apt to try peanut oil. (For the record, peanut oil came in third in my trials.) Spectrum shortening with a smoke point of 450°F, would be my second choice for use on cast iron (using an oven curing temperature of 465°F), but I rest my case in favor of Nutiva organic virgin coconut oil.

(continued)

(continued from p. 215)

DAILY MAINTENANCE

For daily maintenance, all you need are a Lodge scraper, paper towels (or dedicated lint-free cotton towels), and organic virgin coconut oil. After you've cleaned a piece using warm water only, dry it thoroughly. This is important. Or, while it's still wet, give it a quick blast of heat on your stovetop to dry it (don't walk away thinking you'll remember to come back in a moment). If, after having just cooked with it, you feel like it could use a bit of oil, put a "barely there" coating of coconut oil on it, then wipe it off, and you're done. Here's a list of never-evers.

- Never add cold water to an empty pan that's hot. After use, wait for it to cool before using warm water to clean it.

- Never let it soak in water in your sink or bring water to boil in it to loosen food.

- Never put it in your dishwasher.

- Never let it air-dry. Either dry it immediately with a towel or pop it on your stovetop for a quick blast of heat.

"Why I waited all these years to buy a cast-iron skillet, I have no idea. So, I bought two. I can't believe how great they work. I fried up some chicken this morning, made cheeseburgers last night, and last week, made a nice ham chowder. I thought they would be really hard to clean up. But not so. We always used them on the farm I grew up on, so I don't know what I was thinking."
— Nancy Jo Gartenman, MaryJanesFarm chatroom member

QUESTION & ANSWER

Q: I have a chipped piece of enameled cast iron. Can I still use it?
A: If you look closely at a chip, it's surrounded by little shards of what look like glass—the outer coating. If the edges continue to deteriorate, they might end up in your food. There are repair kits available, but they only work if the piece isn't used at higher cooking temperatures. When I come across a chipped piece, I retire it from food by turning it into a storage container, flower vase, or prized collector's item.

Q: Is there a brand of cast iron you recommend?
A: Founded in 1896 by Joseph Lodge, Lodge Manufacturing is one of America's oldest cookware companies still in existence today. Its foundry in Tennessee has kept up with current cookware trends (like their new assist handle) and their products are readily available. Rather than divulge the actual number of Lodge pieces I have, let's just say I'm a good customer of theirs.

216

Le Creuset is a French cookware manufacturer best known for its colorful enameled casseroles and Dutch ovens, which the company calls, you guessed it, "French ovens." Staub is another French company that produces enameled cast iron, most notably the mini cocottes pictured on the back cover. FINEX is an up-and-coming cast-iron manufacturer in Portland, Oregon, specializing in heirloom-quality cookware made in the USA. The octagonal skillet they make is gorgeous. Stargazer, based in Allentown, Pennsylvania, also produces cookware made in the USA. I love the smooth surface on their cookware! Check them out, in addition to Borough Furnace in Syracuse, New York; Marquette Castings in Royal Oak, Michigan; and Smithey Ironworks in Charleston, South Carolina. All of them are exciting, new manufacturers helping to bring back heirloom-quality cast-iron cookware. There are a variety of brands like Camp Chef and Coleman that import cast-iron cookware. If you're going to be using a ceramic stovetop, check first to make sure that what you're thinking about buying doesn't have a raised logo or circular ridge on the bottom of the pan that prevents it from making good contact with your stovetop.

FINEX skillet

Q: Is it true I get a dose of iron whenever I use my cast iron?
A: It depends. If you keep it properly cured, your food isn't coming into direct contact with the cast iron. However, consistently cooking with undiluted acidic foods for prolonged periods of time will strip the curing, resulting in a slightly metallic taste, or without any curing at all, a skillet full of discolored food. In general, a little acidity diluted with other foods is never a problem. Avoid straight doses of lemon juice, vinegar, or wine.

Q: Can I use metal utensils on my cast iron?
A: Yes, of course! Metal spatulas and spoons work fine, but no sharp knives, ever. They'll cut through your layer of curing. In fact, my favorite cast-iron tool is a fine-edged, stainless-steel spatula.

Q: How does cast iron compare to a traditional stainless-steel skillet in terms of heat retention?
A: Cast iron isn't quick to heat up like stainless steel or thin-skinned nonstick pans, but once it's up to temp, it holds the heat much longer. It has very high volumetric heat capacity, which means once it's hot, it stays hot. It also has high emissivity, or heat radiation. In other words, when you're cooking in it, you're not just cooking the food in contact with the metal, but the food above is getting cooked, also. This is important for things like searing meat or roasting a chicken. Cast iron sends its heat in all directions, which is why it's such a joy to use and why it gives you such incredible crusts.

Q: What about cast iron and ceramic stovetops? I've heard you can't use cast iron if you have a ceramic stovetop.
A: In order to dispel that myth, most of the recipes in this book were cooked on a ceramic stovetop. Our first test kitchen had a gas range, but when it came time to get our newest kitchen up and running, we also installed the most commonly sold range, a GE freestanding range from Sears with a ceramic stovetop. Can a test kitchen really be a test kitchen if you use an expensive designer range that's out of reach for most people? We didn't think so.

Vintage cast iron, ready for scrubbing and curing (pp. 212–213) after being put through our oven's self-cleaning cycle (p. 211).

RESOURCES

Here's a lineup of the cast of characters used throughout my book. Even though these pieces are being manufactured today and are readily available for purchase, a good percentage of our recipes use either a skillet or a Dutch oven. If not, a skillet or a Dutch oven can work with a little bit of can-do ingenuity.

8", 10¼", 12" Cast-Iron Skillet

14" Cast-Iron Baking Pan

15" x 12¼" Cast-Iron Rectangular Griddle

10½" Cast-Iron Griddle

4-qt Cast-Iron Universal Pan

Cast-Iron Grill/Griddle

5-qt Cast-Iron Dutch Oven

14" Cast-Iron Wok

9" x 13" Cast-Iron Baking Pan

10" Square Cast-Iron Baking Pan

2-qt Cast-Iron Saucepan

36-oz Cast-Iron Oval Serving Dish
9-oz Cast-Iron Oval Mini-Server

Cast-Iron Aebleskiver Pan

Cast-Iron Wedge Pan

Cast-Iron Cornstick Pan

Cast-Iron Mini Cake Pan

6-Cavity Cast-Iron Muffin Pan

Cast-Iron Loaf Pan

Cast-Iron Waffle Iron

Cast-Iron Breadstick Pan

8" Cast-Iron Tortilla Press

7½" Round Cast-Iron Grill Press

Enameled Cast-Iron Mini
Oval Cocotte

Enameled Cast-Iron Mini
Round Cocotte

Here's the thing about cast iron. It's romantic. It's bold. It's a statement about life the way it should be. Loading a vintage cast-iron bed onto the bed of your farm truck for a romantic getaway in the middle of a field doesn't work if dinner doesn't involve cast-iron cookware and a campfire. When I cook with cast iron in my kitchen, I feel the same way—romantic, emboldened, and somehow defiantly in charge of safeguarding the memory of those before me who, even in the hardest of times, mustered the effort to turn life into a romp.

LIFE ON THE FARM

Piper and Patch were a-frolickin'
Along the road so sweet.
When they thought they heard a cry, a baaa!
Was it their mother, the long-lost sheep?
"Are *you* my mama?" Patch asked.
Maizy, my cow, was all a-bawl.
And with a little spit,
she gave 'em a lick,
"A new auntie," they cried, "so tall!"

"Are *you* my mama?" Piper asked.
"I'll peep and peep all day!"
And with a "cheep"
and a monstrous leap,
The chicken flew away.

But who's *this* working at a desk?
"Baa, baa, baa!" they cried.
"We need a warm lap."

"Now *this* is hopeful," they bellowed,
As my Great Pyrenees, Tulip, said "Hello."
She's big and white …
but not quite right,
One bark and off she went.

And with that, Piper whispered to Patch,
to which she smiled,
"Remember, we have each other."

ACKNOWLEDGMENTS

With my daughter-in-law, Ashley Ogle, by my side, I've managed yet again to turn "play and eat" into a cookbook. With her two daughters, husband, and everyone else at my farm serving as our official food testers, Ashley and I waded through our long list of dream recipes (each one thrice tested). A budding cookbook author in her own right, she's the best kitchen partner I could have. *Thank you, Ashley. I couldn't ask for a more perfect daughter-in-law. There isn't a day goes by that I don't look forward to your good cookin' and kitchen comradery.*

And acknowledging staff photographer/graphic designer/sketch artist Karina Overfelt is bittersweet because after working here five years, she's moving on. This will be her last labor of love with us. Throughout her hitch here, she found a few minutes almost every day to head out the door, camera in hand. Her photos of daily life at my farm and her food photography and artwork throughout this book showcase her wonderful talents. *We'll miss you, Karina. And so will my miniature Jersey milk cow, Lacy Lou* (whose daily milk Ashley turned into the cheeses used throughout this book).

Also, thank you to my daughter, Megan Rae, for content editing; to Carol Hill and Priscilla Wegars for copyediting; and to my four granddaughters, who were willing to smile for our cameras. And thank you to Cydnie Gray, Karina's replacement-in-training. And a hearty *Thank you!* to the men in our family who, without fail, gave us a ravenous thumbs-up on everything we created.

RECIPE INDEX

Brief History of Cast Iron

Cast iron makes me nostalgic. Just the sight of a well-used skillet creates an image of hearty cooks standing before a wood stove in long-ago kitchens. It is said that George Washington's mother so revered her cast-iron cookware that she made special note of it in her will. **Griswold**, founded in 1865 in Erie, Pennsylvania (their first logo was ERIE); **Wagner** (1881, Ohio); **Vollrath** (1874, Wisconsin); **Atlanta Stove Works** (1889, Alabama); and **Wapak** (1903, Ohio) are favorites of collectors.

Like the women in her family before her, MaryJane Butters has always been a pioneer. After graduating from high school in 1971, she was the first woman to attend the Skills Center North Trade School in Ogden, Utah, in carpentry. With a certificate of proficiency in hand, she was hired to build houses at the nearby Hill Air Force Base—the only woman on the crew. From there, she spent her summers watching for fires from a mountaintop lookout in northern Idaho; worked in the Uinta Mountains as one of the first women wilderness rangers in the United States; and in 1976, became the first female station guard at the Moose Creek Ranger Station, the most remote Forest Service district in the continental U.S., in the heart of Idaho's Selway-Bitterroot Wilderness Area. She also built fences in the Tetons of Wyoming, herded cows on the Snake River below Hells Canyon, and raised an organic market garden in White Bird, Idaho.

After moving to her Moscow, Idaho, farm in 1986, she founded a regional environmental group still thriving today (PCEI.org). After four years, she resigned as its director to develop new products for locally grown organic crops that would provide a secure market for farmers transitioning to sustainable production. Along the way, she married her neighbor, Nick Ogle, whose farm borders hers on two sides. Since then, her unique agricultural enterprise has been featured in nearly every major magazine in the country, and in 2008, she was awarded the prestigious Cecil D. Andrus Leadership Award for Sustainability and Conservation. For 14 years, she sponsored an organic farm apprentice program called Pay Dirt Farm School, and for nine years, ran a wall-tent bed and breakfast that she is currently converting to a combination wall-tent/vintage-trailer bed and (outdoor) bath.

Her "everyday organic" lifestyle magazine she launched in 2001, *MaryJanesFarm*, is available nationwide, and she is the author of seven books. She designs her own line of bedding sold in department stores throughout the U.S. and Canada.

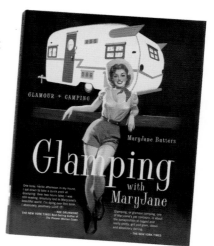

From her farm, she sells 60 different organic prepared foods and shares the message of simple organic living with readers of her magazine and websites (MaryJanesFarm.org, OrganicOnTheGo.org, and RaisingJane.org). In addition, she is the creator of Project F.A.R.M. (First-class American Rural Made), an organization that highlights the businesses of rural women. She is also the owner of the historic four-story Barron Flour Mill. "Nanny" to half-a-dozen grandchildren, MaryJane likes to brag that "going granny" has been her most important accomplishment to date. Two of her grown children and their spouses live and work with her at her farm.

NOTES